Keith Rumjahn

Coaching from the base up

Transformative basketball drills and practice plans from expert coaches

First published by Keith Rumjahn in 2016.

First Edition.

ISBN: 978-988-77649-0-8

This book was professionally typeset on Reedsy.
Find out more at reedsy.com

Contents

Dedication

Dedication

To all the coaches who have shaped my life, thanks!

To Marcus, I couldn't have done it without you.

To my wife, two sons, and my family – thanks for everything!

Foreword

So you've signed up to coach a basketball team for the first time. You've played high school basketball or even at the collegiate level. You have practice coming up soon and you're planning to mix what your coach ran with you back in the day and some drills from YouTube. That was me when I first started coaching a 14-year-old boys' basketball team in Toronto and it didn't work out well for me.

I still cringe thinking about my first season coaching:

- My players were bored during practice. Lots of standing around, waiting, and chatting.
- My players asked me why we did certain drills and I didn't have an answer. There was often no purpose behind the drills.
- I spent a lot of time running our set plays but I didn't feel like players improved skill-wise throughout the season.
- I played my starting five a lot and paid the price later in the season.

Basketball has changed a lot in the past 20 years but practice has remained relatively the same. Since then, I've set out to partner with the best experts in modern basketball coaching to bring you the newest science-backed ideas and drills. Experts such as:

- Bob Bigelow, former NBA player and author of Just Let the

Kids Play.

- Brian McCormick, author of The 21st Century Basketball Practice.
- Chris Oliver, OUA champion coach and creator of Basketball Decision Training and Zero Seconds.
- Don Kelbick, NBA skills coach for Carlos Arroyo and Raja Bell, and the creator of the attack and counter system.
- Ryan Holiday, SMAU and AAU basketball champion and founder of the Next Level Basketball Academy.
- Dell Curry, former NBA player and father of Steph and Seth Curry.
- Steve Collins, three times Wisconsin state champion and founder of Coach Market.
- Joe Riley, Spanish basketball expert and former assistant at Club Estudiantes.

Through our blog (http://blog.coachbase.com) that's read by hundreds of thousands of readers, we've been sharing coaching interviews and drills from each of these experts. If you don't want to miss out, join our growing mailing list at http://blog.coachbase.com/coaching-from-the-base-up-book. We send out a condensed version of our best material every week.

In this book, we hope to give you some fresh ideas such as:

- Why game-based random practices are better than traditional blocked practices.
- Coaching kids is very different from coaching teens, and we list ideas and drills for this specific age group.
- Decision-making ideas and drills that will help your players translate practice moves into game moves.

- Eight common shooting mistakes and how to fix them.

The first part of this book includes extended versions of our interviews with each expert coach, sharing their philosophy behind their coaching and their best drills. The second part is our most popular drills from the practice planner app for shooting, passing, dribbling, and conditioning. The third part is ready-made practice plans from our expert coaches that you can use as a template.

My hope is that this book will stimulate your thinking by bringing together lots of ideas that you may or may not agree with. It's also a very practical book with drills and plans you can use immediately for your next practice. I hope you have a great season!

Only 100 drills are available in this book, but we have over 1300 in total along with videos of each drill inside our practice planner app.

Download the practice planner at http://www.coachbase.com

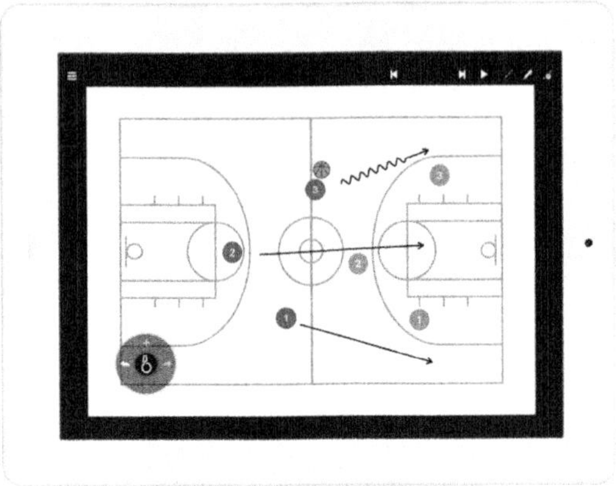

Every drill diagram in this book was drawn using our free Coach's Clipboard app. It can also animate your plays and drills! Trust me, your players will love seeing themselves moving on the screen.

Download the Basketball Coach's Clipboard at http://m.onelink.me/51cfb41c

1

Why games are the best drills

> *"Your child's success or lack of success in sports does not indicate what kind of parent you are, but having an athlete that is coachable, respectful, a great teammate, mentally tough, resilient, and tries their best is a direct reflection of your parenting."*

Brian T. McCormick PhD is a professional basketball coach, consultant, and clinician. McCormick has coached professionally in Denmark, Ireland, and Sweden, and he is the best-selling author of Fake Fundamentals and The 21st Century Basketball Practice as well as a game-based practice expert.

When you think of a typical basketball practice, you conjure up images of players lining up to take a shot one by one. Drills such as the three-man weave that look controlled and are executed to perfection every time.

Coach McCormick discusses why random game-based practices yield better results for player development and why the three-man weave teaches fake skills that don't translate to games no matter how many times you do it.

Breaking down coaching myths

Using games to build fundamentals instead of thinking of fundamentals and skills that shouldn't cross.

Myth: you must break down and isolate skills first

For many people, it is natural to think that you must break down skills into simpler components and progressively load the drills. For example, starting from a stationary dribble, you work your way up to a walking dribble, and then onto a running dribble.

On the other end of the spectrum, you have an uncontrolled no rules five v five game. Coach McCormick argues that the ideal environment for skill acquisition and retention lies somewhere in between using games with specific task constraints.

Research has shown that games are better for skill acquisition and motor learning, as it leads to better transfer and retention. Transfer is the ability to transfer a practice skill into a game skill. If a player shoots 90 percent in practice and 90 percent in game then there is perfect transfer. Retention is the ability to recall the learned skill after a period of no practice – i.e. players are able to retain their skills from one practice session to the next.

For example: dribbling. Instead of building up from stationary dribbling and pound dribbles, Coach McCormick suggests playing tag dribbling. This forces the players to look up and react to a defender while constraining the task to just dribbling.

Myth: personal training is better than street ball

Since 2011, Coach McCormick has stopped doing private training. He spent many years doing one-on-one tuition and some of his players even went on to play professionally. However, the problem is that he didn't think this kind of tuition was an effective way to develop real game skills. Even with two players doing the same workouts, one would go on to play pro while the other didn't improve much. The blame was often placed on a person's athleticism or talent, but not on the training method itself.

Coach McCormick now believes that playing pickup games is better for player development. He's seen that players become aware of their weaknesses. For example, Coach McCormick couldn't score against taller players and so he would find new ways to get results, such as working on his floater and runners.

"Everything is so regimented and adult supervised," said McCormick, commenting on the state of basketball today. Current training methods stifle creativity because players are always following demonstrations and not creating their own. For example: scoring one-on-one in transition is less about skill and more about decision-making. On a fast break, a hesitation may already be enough and you don't need a crossover every time.

Another example is the Euro step. Lots of players will now default to using the Euro step when it's suppose to be a counter. Learning when to use it can only be achieved through games because you can't read defense on a one-on-zero scenario.

Myth: three-man weave is a great passing drill

To understand why Coach McCormick thinks certain drills are not effective, we have to explain the three different types of transfer in motor learning. The transfer of learning is defined as how practice skills transfers to game performance.

POSITIVE TRANSFER – leads to better performance in games.

ZERO TRANSFER – no difference in performance between games and practice.

NEGATIVE TRANSFER – leads to worse performance in games.

Coach McCormick points out that the three-man weave is a poor passing drill and is either a zero transfer or negative transfer skill. Why?

- You strive perfect execution in the drill, which never happens in a game.
- No defenders. Most bad passes are caused by defenders.
- Low repetition. On each trip, players don't actually get a lot of passing opportunities.

Myth: shell drills are great for team defense

There is certainly a place for team defense and shell drills but Coach McCormick argues that below the age of nine the natural instinct is just to crowd the ball so help defense will most likely come. This is an example of a negative transfer skill where players are taught to stay on their man then later taught to pack the middle on help later, which can be confusing. It is better to just focus on one-on-one defense first at a very young age.

How to design drills for your practices

Now that we've gone through what not to do, Coach McCormick will go into specific drills that are better for player development. He believes that you should start with having only three goals for your entire season. McCormick's three goals for youth players are:

- Ability to dribble comfortably.
- Ability to layup off one and two feet (normal layups, inside hand, reverse).
- Ability to guard one-on-one.

For example: two v two rugby. Coach McCormick plays a two v two full-court game where the offense can only pass backward. This forces the players to apply all three principles that he wants to enforce that season. To determine what you want to work on, ask yourself if you only had 10 minutes a day, what would you work on? Two v two rugby is one of those drills.

Practice planning for first-time coaches

Process of preparing for practice makes you better prepared.

Here are some tips for beginner coaches:

- Plan every practice. The process itself is useful.
- Keep spare drills incase there's low energy.
- Keep a record after every practice on how to improve.

Coach McCormick used to write all his practices on index cards and planned it minute by minute. After each practice, he would write about what went wrong and what went right. This allowed him to look back to see how much time he had spent on different drills and where he could improve.

He also suggests having backup drills such as a fun drill when energy is down and extra drills if they go faster than expected. The most important part about planning practice is the process of planning itself. If you find yourself doing the same drills three weeks in a row, come up with new ones.

How to design small-sided games

You can use small-sided games with constraints to work on different skills. If you want to work on conditioning, three-on-three full-court is a great conditioning drill. If you want to work on pick and roll, you can start each possession in a pick and roll position. Changing the starting position to force a constraint in a drill is a great way to teach specific offensive/defensive concepts.

If you want to work on passing and force players to make decisions before catching the ball, you can play keep away. In this, players cannot hold the ball for more than one second. Coach McCormick noticed that US players play at a much slower pace than their European counterparts because there is a tendency to hold the ball. Players should anticipate and make decisions before catching the ball.

If you want to work on rebounding, give a point for every offensive rebound. To simulate pressure, introduce a constraint to make two free throws in a row when a team wins a game. If they can't hit both, the game restarts.

How to encourage creativity

First of all, Brian McCormick always says: "If you're making mistakes, you're not working hard enough." Practice is time to expand skill level, so get that mentality right from the start. One of the ways to improve creativity is to force players to think. For example, Brian asks his players to do layup lines but the constraint is that you cannot finish the same way as the person in front of you. So you can use reverse, Euro step, one footed, two footed, inside hand. Same with pick and roll. Players must use a different screen every time - off ball screen, flare, or curl.

For example, Coach McCormick asks his players to do layup lines but the constraint is that they cannot finish the same way as the person in front of them. This drill brings out reverse, Euro step, one footed, two footed, inside hand layups. The same can be done with the pick and roll. Run a five-on-five but players must use a different screen to receive the ball every time. You'll soon be seeing plenty of off-ball screens, flares, and curls. The great thing about drills where players get to make decisions is that they'll soon figure out what works best for them. These are skills that are likely to transfer into games.

Quick summary: Sometimes, rules can be used in ways to force players to be creative.

Overall summary

Perfect progressions don't translate into games – only 'messy' drills where your players make decisions and mistakes do. Small-sided games are the answer to creating drills with a positive transfer to actual games. Be wary of over teaching with younger players – focus on individual fundamentals first. Your drills need to match the player development goals that you have in mind. Ask yourself if each drill has a purpose. Use rules to turn small-sided games into drills that can teach specific skills and concepts without hindering decision-making.

2

Just let the kids play

A recent study by the National Alliance for Sports shows that a shocking 70 percent of American kids are dropping out of sport by the age of 13. There is a huge disconnect between the children who play sports and the parents and coaches who organize it. What's even more bizarre is the reason why kids play the game is so blatantly out there, yet so many adults choose to ignore it. It can be summed up in one short word – FUN.

Unfortunately, coaches often neglect fun in favor of chasing success. Think about these commonly employed strategies and ask yourself, "do they really make the game fun for the kids on my team?":

- Playing the best starting five for most of the game.
- Getting angry with the referee, or worse, your players.
- Cutting players from a team.
- Running set plays on offense and benching players for not following them.
- Making young players do drills that they are not physically ready for.

Granted, these strategies may have a place in high school, collegiate, or professional basketball, but at the elementary school level they will only stunt a young player's development and turn them off playing the game. Anyone who has seen an elementary or middle school match can observe that success is largely determined by one factor – height. Shorter players have yet to develop enough skills or experience to overcome these physical disadvantages. Kids are continually developing physically and mentally into their early twenties but you will never know if a late bloomer could achieve something in basketball if they quit the sport when there were young. This is why Bob Bigelow, former NBA player and current youth basketball advocate, argues that we must "just let the kids play" in order for them to achieve their fullest potential as basketball players.

Quick summary: if you are an elementary or middle school coach, create a program that makes players think: "yes, I want to come back here next year!"

Since retiring from the NBA after a career that included playing under Hall of Fame coach Chuck Daly, Bob Bigelow has spent his time researching and teaching strategies to coach youth basketball. He's written several books about the subject, including the aptly titled Just Let the Kids Play, and we were fortunate enough to learn from him in an exclusive interview conducted in 2016. While our interview focused on largely positive things that coaches could do, it's worth briefly outlining what Coach Bigelow views as 'coaching sins' in today's game:

1. **Adults being far too focused on winning at the expense**

of meeting children's needs. This goes back to the earlier studies we referenced regarding a difference between what children want from basketball (fun), and what adults tend to push for (winning). Coach Bigelow goes further and argues that "more games, tournaments and playoffs do not make for better kids' sports. More emphasis on learning new skills, participation, fun, and properly managed competition is what keeps them coming back!"

2. **Parents and coaches that behave in inappropriate and even downright abusive ways.** The occurrence of such behavior is the natural progression from caring too much about winning. These behaviors, aside from turning kids off the game, set a poor example for them to follow. A basketball coach must remember that young children are particularly impressionable and their role is to not just teach the game, but to teach good attitudes for life.
3. **Children are overspecializing at younger ages, leading to injury.** By warning against overspecializing, Coach Bigelow is advocating principles of the Long-Term Athlete Development (LTAD) model designed by Canada Basketball (for more information, turn to page 66). Younger players are increasingly being asked to focus solely on basketball from younger ages, and the repetitive strain on muscles and joints is leading to injury. On the flip side, there is good evidence from Canada Basketball's model that encouraging kids to play many sports leads to the development of vital motor skills that readily transfer into basketball.

Quick summary: being too focused on winning, bad behavior, and overspecializing too early are three major mistakes youth coaches make. Avoid them at all costs.

How you can make a difference

Now that you know about the three situations to avoid when coaching kid's basketball, the question becomes: how can I, as a youth coach, help create a fun environment where my players can develop their basketball skills? Our interview with Coach Bigelow yielded several gems. We start with how you plan a practice – what you should be teaching and which drills you decide to use. We then talk about specific adjustments you can make in games and during practice, which will ultimately shift the focus from winning to developing. Finally, we talk about dealing with difficult parents and how to get them to 'buy in' to your philosophy.

Planning a basketball practice for 5–10-year-olds

Selecting the right equipment

The all-encompassing principle that Coach Bigelow introduced to us in his interview was the idea that "coaches should seek to adapt the game to the kids, and never the kids to the game." To illustrate his point to other coaches, Coach Bigelow uses several striking examples. One of them is getting coaches at his clinics to do simple basketball drills such as layups and dribbling with a 9 lb (4.1 kg) medicine ball. The weight of the four kg medicine ball to adults, Coach Bigelow argues, is what the full sized 29.5 in (75 cm), 22 oz (0.6 kg) ball is to kids. After watching these adults, it becomes apparent that maintaining good technique for any length of time is impossible.

Another great example of poor equipment choices is the issue of shooting on a 10-ft hoop. For too long, we have been getting our young players to shoot on hoops that are too high for their current capabilities. Coach Bigelow illustrates this with the example of trying to shoot on a 20-ft hoop, roughly the height of a basketball hoop when it is raised and stored away in a gym. Anyone who has tried to shoot when it this high will soon adopt bad habits, like shooting from the hip, yet this is the equivalent height we expect our 3-ft-tall kids to shoot at!

Clearly there is a need to adapt the equipment to the physical capabilities of younger players, yet basketball is often unfortunately lagging in this area. In other sports, such as baseball or soccer, playing with adapted equipment has become the standard for coaching and competitions, not the exception. Adapting the equipment starts with the following areas, as advocated by Coach Bigelow:

1. Play with smaller basketballs

Rather than using the 29.5 in size seven ball, Coach Bigelow recommends a size five ball for kids under the age of 10. This ball weighs only 17 oz compared with 22 oz, and the reduced weight and size will allow your kids to control the ball better. A general rule of thumb is that when kids are able to shoot a one-handed shot from 10 ft (3 m) with a size seven ball with no noticeable loss of form, they're strong enough to use it.

2. Use 8- or 9-ft (2.4–2.7 m) rims

Isn't it ridiculous that a 6 ft 7 in (2 m) giant like LeBron James is using the same 10-ft (3-m) high rims as many eight-year-olds around the country? If your facilities allow you to, your U8 kids should be using 8-ft (2.4-m) rims, and your U10s 9-ft (2.7-m) rims. This will allow them to practice proper shooting form right from the start.

3. Embrace smaller courts and smaller games (three-on-three)

Reducing the size and number of players on the court has many benefits. The obvious point is that with fewer people to share the basketball with, each player will benefit from getting more touches of the ball. That means more time to practice passes, shooting, and dribbling. Young players also tend to play the game at a frenetic pace, often doing more running than playing basketball in full-court games. Players will find it easier to score in a smaller game so they'll learn to make use of each possession.

4. Have more balls than kids

A good youth practice will involve plenty of fundamentals training (more on this later) – drills that can be done individually, under the eye of a coach. Giving everyone a ball helps keep the kids focused on a task. It's a no-brainer that your players will improve faster if doing a drill rather than standing around.

Quick summary: the key pointers you need to prepare for your next youth training session are: 1. Smaller basketballs 2. Lower rims 3. Use smaller games 4. Have more balls than kids.

What's a fundamental?

What skills should a U8 or U10 coach REALLY be teaching? According to Coach Bigelow, there are too many coaches out there who believe that learning to shoot fade ways or teaching the full-court press are 'fundamentals.' In actuality, the most basic fundamental a coach should teach is movement skills. (Not surprisingly, this idea is echoed by Team Canada on page 67). The basic errors that plague a U10 game – travelling, double dribbles, and losing control of the ball – are all due to the lack of coordination in young players.

There is no quick fix to teach movement skills. Coach Bigelow notes that this process can take up to five or six years – well into middle school. Yet the foundations must be laid at the youth level. As you'll see later, many of Coach Bigelow's drills emphasize footwork and high coordination, with drills as simple yet vital as teaching the one-two layup step, defensive slides, and how to pivot.

It's also worth noting that the lack of physical strength in young players affects what skills can be taught. Coach Bigelow points out that dribbling is done with gravity, while passing is done along it, and shooting is done completely against gravity. A simple factor like this can make drills for kids much harder than originally conceived. Hence, many of Coach Bigelow's drills focus on ball handling – there's no excuse to not teach handles from a young age. Your kids should also always pass with two hands for control and you need to favor teaching layups over jump shots. Your kids may miss open layups but that'll often be due to a lack of strength and hand-eye coordination. Focus instead on the things that they can control – did they pick the ball up correctly, did they use the correct hand, did they avoid travelling? With this knowledge in mind you'll find yourself much less stressed about the results and focusing more on their technique.

Quick summary: the teaching order of fundamentals goes: 1. Movement skills 2. Dribbling 3. Passing 4. Close shooting. That's it!

Structuring a practice

There are two significant differences between teaching teenagers and kids that drastically affect how you should plan a practice for young people. The first difference is intuitive to any parent –kids have short attention spans and need more motivation than adults to stay focused. The second difference is equally important but not so obvious – kids get tired much quicker than adults. A bunch of hyperactive children can quickly become tired and listless if pushed too hard for too long. The consequences of both situations are that you will find the kids near impossible to manage.

Coach Bigelow's secret to getting around this is to use children's hardwired disposition for short bursts of energy to form exciting, high-energy practice plans. Here is how a general practice plan of his is structured, and why:

1. Practice for no more than one hour

Kids will tire after an hour, even if given rest breaks. It is better to keep the practice short and sweet, and send the kids home wanting to come back for more.

2. Structure practice sessions like this: 20 minutes of individual training, 20 minutes of small-sided games, the rest for three-on-three.

This is how Coach Bigelow balances time spent teaching individual fundamentals with time teaching team skills. In the 20 minutes of individual training, everyone should have a ball to maximize time on task. Small-sided games are game-based drills that focus on a particular skill – it can be particularly hard to think of some for young kids so definitely check out our appendix for ideas. Finally, half-court three-on-three is the best way to apply the skills taught in a game.

3. Limit each drill to five minutes

By this, we mean time spent doing the drill, so including two-three minutes for explanations means that you'll be switching over to something new every seven or eight minutes. The reason for this is to take advantage of kid's high initial enthusiasm for new drills to get them training at 100 percent. As you'll see from Coach Bigelow's practice plans, this will add up to roughly six drills a practice, including time for a break and a short game at the end.

4. No more than two focuses a practice

Having fewer focuses helps your kids build off earlier skills, and also makes it easier for you to plan as a coach. Try to make sure your small-sided games complement both these skills. For example, if your focuses are dribbling and defense, a great small-sided game would be dribble tag, where your players have to try to steal other players' balls. Other focuses could be shooting, passing, team offense, finishing, and rebounding.

Quick summary: the key points for structuring a kid's practice are: 1. Short one-hour practice sessions. 2. Split them into 20 min of individual/20 min of small-sided games/rest on three-on-three, with a rest break. 3. Plan for around six drills of seven or eight minutes each. 4. Select one or two focuses for each practice session.

Key details to pay attention to

Although your players will be making more mistakes, that doesn't mean that you, as a coach, should be careless. In fact, it was clear talking to Coach Bigelow about the intricacies of the youth game that a kid's basketball coach needs an even BETTER attention to detail. Why? Your job is to be focused on the process, not the results. Often, you'll need to wade through a torrent of mistakes to pick out the one great thing that your kids did. Never underestimate the importance of praise - if you manage to show them that one bright spot it'll give them something to remember and build off the next time they play. We've listed some notable observations by Coach Bigelow to keep in mind for your next practice or game.

What to keep in mind in practice

Stick with your players through their mistakes

Bob Bigelow suggests that you be "very laudatory with your kids, constantly pump them up - tell them that they're doing great, doing things a little better than they did last time." His reasoning behind seemingly excessive praise is simple: young kids are bound to make tons of mistakes early on, but five years down the line, if – and only if – they're still interested in basketball, they can start developing into good players. In fact, the biggest kids, the ones that will likely have the most success in basketball later on, are likely to be the clumsiest when they first start. On the other hand, punishing them for making mistakes by shouting at them or benching them will only discourage them from playing.

Learning to love the game of basketball starts with a player's first coach. Telling players that they're doing great and encouraging them to work hard for the reward a few years down the line can go a long way toward getting your young players to love the game.

Quick summary: eight-year-old kids can only become great 18-year-old players if they're still playing the game

Learn from other sports

Even a youth coach expert like Coach Bigelow has found it difficult to find good practice ideas for coaching U5s to U11s. The reason is that he finds many coaches are either too focused on winning or have the wrong idea of what to teach. Instead of looking at your peers, Coach Bigelow suggests you turn to youth coaches in other areas, such as lacrosse, soccer, or hockey. He has found that sports like these are often miles ahead of basketball when it comes to introducing their game to younger players. Many of the drills that they use to introduce skills are often applicable to basketball. Other great resources are P.E. coaches – professionals at teaching sports to youngsters. They are often taught to view sports from a movement skills basis first, which can be a refreshing and useful point of view. Finally, some coaches are beginning to realize the need for resources at the youth level – for example the Practice Planner app with all of Coach Bigelow's drills inside is a great place to start!

Quick summary: try looking for inspiration from other sports and P.E. teachers for your next practice.

What to watch in games

Measure success in ways other than points scored

According to Bob Bigelow, "In any youth basketball team, you will have children able to score more than other children, that's the way it goes. With that said, what can you do as a coach to help kids on your team who don't score as many points, or don't score any points, feel like they're part of the action?" Rebounds and assists are the two other most obvious stats to track, but because of the nature of basketball, it's often the most developed players that get the rebounds as well as the points, and meanwhile as there are so many missed shots, assists are far and few between. Here are some less obvious stats that you need to be recording:

- **Keeping track of screens set.** Often, setting a screen frees up another player for an easy score but is otherwise unrewarded. Try giving players a point for each screen they set. "It's amazing when you do this how often kids will set screens, simply because they get points," Bigelow observes.

- **Keep track of consecutive passes.** Try recording consecutive passes that a team makes in a possession. Reward teams with points for making two or more consecutive passes. The reason behind giving reward for such a seemingly mundane stat is that "you don't want to just reward the kids for effort and trying, but you want to give them some tangible things that they can try to do: making better passes, setting picks, helping out team mates."
- **Keep track of players that have a hand up when defenders take a shot.** "Even if that shot goes in", says Coach Bigelow, "and some of them will, reward that player for trying to make the other player shoot a little worse."

The fact that even NBA teams will record stats like these shows that there are many more aspects to basketball than just counting points. One other benefit of keeping track of all these stats as a coach is that you can assign these jobs to other parents, keeping them off your back and out of the referee's face!

Quick summary: don't just focus on the score – track the little things such as screens, passes, and defensive hustles as well.

Try taking a seat in your next game

"When you see coaches on TV – major college and NBA games – don't watch what those coaches are doing," Bob Bigelow implores youth basketball coaches. Why should youth coaches sit down and stop standing up? Firstly, from his experience, coaches who stand talk "five to 10 times more than coaches that are sitting," which is a natural result of standing. More importantly, coaches who stand get a better view of the court, see mistakes players make, and also see what their players aren't seeing. They forget in situations like this that not only is their player not as tall as they are, but they are also being guarded by several players of the same height. In situations like this, if you're interested in helping your players Bob Bigelow suggests to ask them what they saw. "You may not like the answer," he says, "because it's not what you saw. But the reason you saw it was because you stood up and got a panorama of 10 players on the floor, which they will never see."

Moreover, the pace of basketball dictates that within a matter of seconds, the player with the ball will see the nine other players in completely different positions. Even higher-level players – college and professionals – struggle to see everything and take all of this in. While a coach can pause the practice to point out what they should have done, when young kids get into the playing environment and feel the excitement of the game they can easily forget things. Instead of trying to correct things that your players won't see, sit down and let them learn from their mistakes.

Quick summary: listen to Coach Bigelow and just let the kids play.

Getting the parents to buy in

One last word is needed on how to get the parents of your players to buy into your system. There are parents who wholeheartedly believe that their kid is the next NBA phenomenon and think that you're not pushing them hard enough. Others will be cheering and jeering at the sideline like it's game seven of the NBA playoffs. They might be doing it for the right reasons, but unfortunately the pressure that these parents put on their kids is often the number one reason why they end up quitting the sport when they get old enough to make their own decisions.

The following list is the '10 Commandments for Basketball Parents' that we posted on our website that absolutely blew up. We figured that it was an important message for parents to hear, so we've included it here. You should share this with players' parents at the start of every season.

1. Thou shalt not impose your ambitions on thy child
Remember that basketball is your child's activity. In a sport where size does matter, and uneven growth is a reality, don't judge your child's performance based on the performances of others.

2. Thou shalt be supportive no matter what
Children play to have fun. Don't ruin it for them.

3. Thou shalt not coach thy child
By signing your child up to a team, you have entrusted their development to a coach. Let them focus on your child's

technique and learning. Coaching your child will confuse them and undermine the coach-player bond.

4. Thou shalt only have positive things to say at a game
Cheer and applaud, but never criticize the coach.

5. Thou shalt acknowledge thy child's fears
Being nervous and under performing at a game is a difficulty only the child can overcome. Don't make it worse by belittling them.

6. Thou shalt not criticize the officials
Basketball is a game played by humans. Everyone makes mistakes. They are not refereeing at the NBA finals.

7. Honor thy child's coach.
The coach-player bond is a special and important one for player growth and fun. Don't tarnish it by criticizing the coach in front of your child.

8. Thou shalt respect thy child's teammates
The players around your child are learning the game as well. Don't impart a bad attitude to your child by blaming or criticizing them.

9. Thy child shall have goals other than winning
Playing your hardest and never giving up is more important than winning. These attitudes go a lot further than a single basketball game.

10. Thou shalt not expect your child to play in the NBA (or

even college!)

As many as one in 35 (3.6 percent) of high school players end up on a college team. The chance of making an NBA team is even smaller at three in 10,000. Reaching the highest levels of play is an opportunity few get, but it doesn't stop people from competing and having fun. Basketball can teach discipline, build character, instill a healthy lifestyle, and help your child make lifelong friends. Everyone, no matter their skill level, can gain these benefits by playing. Let's keep the game fun!

Summary

- Your job as a youth basketball coach is to create a fun environment where players want to learn, get better, and come back to play again and again.
- Winning isn't the most important thing at this level – don't let the desire to win affect your behavior.
- Make sure you adapt the game to the kids, not the kids to the game. Use smaller balls, hoops, and courts, and organize games with fewer players to maximize touches.
- Movement skills are the number one fundamental. Learning plays are not!
- Structure a practice knowing that your kids perform best in short bursts. Keep the intensity high but for short periods of time.
- In practices, stick with your players through their mistakes and don't be afraid to learn from other sports.
- In games, relax and turn the focus on anything other than winning. Focus on the little things because they are what will stick in the future. Kids can only become great at basketball if they stick with the game until adulthood.

Make sure parents remember that as well.

3

Taking player development to the Next Level

I interviewed Coach Ryan Holliday, founder of Next Level Basketball, to provide you with the essential principles of designing a skill-focused development program.

An Amateur Athletic Union (AAU) Coach, Coach Holliday has designed an effective skills training system for his middle school teams. The four key principles to keep in mind as you design workouts for your players are Vision, Preparation, Progression, and Patience.

Do you want to always be organized? How do you decide which is the 'right' area for players to develop next? What is the secret behind the attention to detail that coaches so crave?

It all starts with these four principles:

1. Vision – to see what players can't.
2. Preparation – to be ready for what players aren't.
3. Progression – to know what to do next when players don't.
4. Patience – to pause when players haven't.

In case you didn't notice, none of these four principles just happen – they all start with prior knowledge gained from practice planning. Hopefully, we'll give you the knowledge to apply them to your players. These four principles will now be explored in some depth.

Vision

It is important to envision both the bigger picture and the finer details of your player's basketball skills. Coach Holliday takes inspiration from legendary college coach Bobby Knight, who says that, "the best coaches have eyes that see the details of the game." Every day in practice, a coach must be able to draw upon his experience and knowledge of the game to see things on the court that a player will not have noticed. This knowledge, Coach Holliday notes, can come from one's own experience as a player, but also from watching the game – whether it be on TV or sitting in on practice sessions of other coaches. Don't worry if you haven't played basketball professionally or even in college – playing experience at the highest level hasn't always made people great coaches (see, for example, Magic Johnson and Bill Russell). What's truly important is the persistence to constantly be around the game and the curiosity to ask: how can I use this to make my players better?

Coach Holliday also says that "You must be able to see with your eyes and turn those thoughts into words that affect a player's skill development." A coach must carefully watch a player's footwork, shooting form, anticipation skills, etc., and then be able to suggest improvements. However, a coach must first have a reference point of the 'correct' form in his mind. Watching videos, reading books, attending camps, and speaking to great players are a few of the many things you can do to understand what the perfect form really is. Once again, we see that vision really is derived from solid preparation.

Quick summary: having an eye for the game starts with preparation.

In addition, a coach must also analyze a player's goals and potential to come up with a vision of the 'final product.' He must give the player technical corrections to help mold them to be that player. One story Coach Holliday told is that after noticing one of his eighth grade players had a low shot release, he then set about trying to make that shot release higher. Although this player was making shots at the eighth grade level, Coach Holliday saw that his release would inhibit his potential to be a great college player. He then taught him a series of drills so that he could eventually develop a college-level jump shot. Sometimes, coaches can be afraid of changing something as fundamental as a player's shot – if it works now, why change it and risk them not being able to make it in games? As a coach, you are like a CEO. While all of your players are only focused on the next game, you must always have one eye on the future. The will to change starts with you, and must be the strongest with you.

Quick summary: player development starts with the coach... and never ends. Always look ahead.

Preparation

Often, enthusiasm alone is not enough to develop a young player. Coach Holliday notes how he often sees countless parents trying to teach their kids shooting form, only to give them bad habits that ultimately become harder to correct. Moreover, a young player left to their own devices often just wants to learn flashy crossovers and long threes, taking on skills that are too complex for their level or will be useless in a game.

Without a doubt, a coach's job when developing a player must be to reign in these tendencies and get them building their skills from the base up. At the Next Level Basketball Academy, Coach Holliday preaches three essential offensive skills for middle school players (11–14 years old):

1. Dribbling and finishing at the rim – ideally taught from a young age.
2. Shooting – middle school is also the time when players are strong enough to learn perfect shot form. This is then used to develop an outside as well as the 'lost art' of the midrange game.
3. Post moves – finally, Coach Holliday also believes in teaching all players, regardless of size, post moves. This develops them into fully rounded offensive players and works on fundamental skills such as footwork and finishing.

Practicing these offensive fundamentals allows players to develop an all-round offensive game, with the ability to score from inside, the midrange, and from beyond the perimeter. The idea that all players must be a threat to score from wherever they catch the basketball is fundamental to the modern game and is an idea that both Coach Holliday and Coachbase stands by.

Quick summary: dribbling and finishing, shooting, and post moves are the three vital offensive skills a middle school coach must pass onto his players.

To be prepared to teach these three skills, a coach must have hundreds of drills available and the knowledge to execute those drills perfectly.

Why are these two ingredients essential to success? Firstly, as Coach Holliday told us, having a litany of drills is useful when it comes to correcting errors in technique. Secondly, as players inevitably develop they will need to learn increasingly challenging drills. When it comes to the drills themselves, coaches not only need to know the basics, such as the equipment and how to run it, but also where common errors might occur or what variations to run if players find the drills too easy or too difficult. Few resources offer the range and depth a coach needs, so definitely try everything – books, websites, camps, and basketball apps.

Quick summary: don't let player development by limited by your lack of drill knowledge.

Progression

Coach Holliday told us that he believes that players must first repeat a move 500 times in a solo work out before it is ready to be used in practice. Even then, from his experience it takes another 500 repetitions with defense before that move can even be used in a game situation. If a player wants to improve, it is his or her responsibility to practice by himself, but it's the coach's responsibility to provide them with a detailed training plan.

Team Next Level runs individual drills in the form of high intensity skill circuits in practice, which is when coaches can observe players and give feedback. These drills then form the basis for individual take-home workouts that coaches assign to players. Take a look at the table for the 'killer crossover' workout below as an example. The great thing about this method is that 1. Players start off being taught with the correct technique; and 2. When the drill is repeated in practice a few weeks later, coaches will know if they have really worked on it and can issue appropriate feedback.

Quick summary: individual drills in practice should become drills to take home.

Killer crossover workout
In and out dribbling drill – two minutes.
Single crossovers – two minutes.
In and out crossovers – two minutes.
Double crossover dribbling – two minutes.
Double tap crossovers – two minutes.

Front rakes dribbling drill – two minutes.
Cross-between-behind drill – two minutes.
Triple tap crossovers – two minutes.
Behind the back dribbling drill – two minutes.
Baby steps crossover – two minutes.
In and out cone-to-cone – two minutes.
In and out cone-to-cone crossovers – two minute.
Exaggerated cone-to-cone crossover drill – two minutes.
Next level crossovers – two minutes.

The right progression must be carefully chosen to allow for success. Coach Holliday breaks each skill down into dozens of different drills, each of which, when repeated many times, builds the final move. For example, in the killer crossover series he's designed a progression of 15 dribbling drills that make up a half-hour workout.

The key to progression is that each drill is only slightly more difficult than the last. The principle here is that there is only one focus (teaching the crossover), but many drills are performed, each teaching a specific sub focus. Each exercise slowly works up toward building an additional aspect of the 'killer crossover.' Something that separates Coach Holliday from many other coaches is that each progression starts from the most basic form. That means the players start off with static dribbling exercises, crossing over the ball in front of them at knee height. There is no other movement, no between the legs or behind the back technique – the focus is entirely on their coordination skills and arm strength. Next, movement and footwork is gradually added. Finally, players are ready to integrate their crossover with other skills, such as finishing and shooting. The result is that players develop every aspect of that skill and are not just learning a singular move.

Apply this 'bottom up' principle into your own individual training plans by remembering that higher level skills are by definition more complex and need to be eased into. Teach three-point shooting? Then start the progression with a form shooting drill 5 ft (1.5 m) from the basket. Teaching a post-drop step should start from a basic drill like the Mikan; finishing with the Euro step might start with drilling a one-dribble pick-up into a layup. If you're not sure where to start, we've got many more individual progressions designed by Coach Holliday that you can use to get inspired!

Quick summary: think of the end goal as a point on a graph and each drill as a data point. You want a smooth curve to the goal – don't make your players jump up huge steps!

Patience

Developing new skills takes time and dedication. Coach Holliday holds his players accountable to wanting to be better basketball players. For example, he expects his middle school players to work on a dribbling series for at least 20 minutes, three times a week. Each Next Level basketball player must first sign an agreement to confirm their commitment to the program and becoming a better player. As a coach, if you're going to the trouble of designing individual workouts, your players have the responsibility to see that they are completed.

One caveat however – it's important that each workout

presents your player with a realistic and attainable challenge. Nothing disheartens a young player more than repeated failure. As much as we talk about never giving up, if a player is clanking three after three, or losing the handle every 10 seconds, then that is down to you for giving them something that they clearly aren't ready for. In fact, even if they don't give up they'll likely start developing bad habits such as looking down when dribbling or poor shooting form to compensate. The principle of preparation is therefore vital.

Quick summary: set realistic goals for your players to work toward each day.

Aside from demanding dedication, Coach Holliday also believes in the importance of letting players fail. One of the most enlightening ideas from his interview with Coachbase was when he talked about how hard it is to push players to try something new in a game. Often, players will play using only the skills they are comfortable with, as they'll be afraid of looking silly or getting benched. To combat this attitude, he give his players goals such as "I want you to go to the low block and use X move I taught you and score with it at least three times this game", etc. It's after trying the move and persevering until finding success with it that players become more comfortable at regularly using it in games. Rather than benching players for failure, Coach Holliday knows that games at the middle school level are not about winning but about developing skills.

Quick summary: players will only use their new skills in games if they know that you've got their backs – always be clear to communicate this.

Key points

- AAU basketball, when coached well, is a great opportunity for players to develop individual skills.
- Vision, preparation, progression, and patience – these are the four principles for developing a successful individual player development program.
- A coach's vision in practice is developed by gaining experience and knowledge about the game from it.
- The three key offensive skills to prepare for are dribbling and finishing, shooting and posting up.
- Have the end goal in mind and put together a progression of incrementally difficult drills to build up to it. Start from the most basic!

Your hard work and good communication will empower your players to take the steps that they need to develop their skills.

4

Basketball decision training and zero seconds

Chris Oliver is head coach for the Canadian University of Windsor's Men's Lancers, an elite college team that competes against NCAA-level competition and winner of three Ontario University Athletic championships. What's different about Chris Oliver is that he's a self-taught coach who never played professionally or even at the collegiate level.

We start off by asking how often do your players have to make split-second decisions during a game? The answer is 'lots.' But how many traditional drills incorporate decision training? Apparently not a lot.

In this interview, Coach Oliver introduces two concepts he developed and how you can incorporate these into your existing drills:

- Zero seconds – how to train your players to attack off the catch immediately and increase the speed of your offense.
- Basketball decision training – how to incorporate decision training into your drills.

"Zero seconds training is about teaching skills; basketball decision training is about teaching knowledge."
– Chris Oliver

What's the zero seconds concept and why should I use it?

If you look at the Warriors and the Spurs, how often do they pause/hold onto the ball or take a jab step? The answer is almost never. They almost always shoot, penetrate, or pass the ball – this is zero seconds. They've already decided what to do before they even catch the ball, as opposed to many players who catch the ball and then decide what to do afterwards, which slows down the offense. Too many players catch the ball to pass the ball. Not enough players are ready to shoot or make a decision.

The two core tenants of zero seconds are:

1. You'll never be more open than the moment you catch the ball.
2. It is never wrong to shoot an open shot.

Coach Oliver believes that it's important players catch the ball with the primary intention to shoot. If the shot is not open, players must read the defense and make a decision immediately, i.e. within 0 seconds. He believes that the only thing preventing a player from shooting should be the defense. In reality, though, coaches and even the players themselves often prevent themselves from taking open shots. Permitting players to shoot when open does a few positive things to your mindset:

- Players feel more confident because the coach is empowering their decisions.

- There's more freedom and room for players to make decisions.
- It prevents over coaching from the sideline in games.

Note that giving your players the green light in games comes with a caveat – your players have to earn that 'right' in practice. That comes with many responsibilities, including showing up to practice and working on your jump shot and listening to the coach's feedback in training. There's a fine line between player development and wanting to win at middle school and older levels, but we would tend to put the focus on attitude over results, especially earlier on. You shouldn't expect your players to drain shots from three like Steph Curry, but provided they made the right decision and have shown that that's a shot they work hard on in practice, we'd argue that that's a shot they should be taking in a game.

Quick summary: the zero seconds concept is about making a decision as soon as you catch the ball, and it starts with being ready to shoot.Zero seconds is being able to play without a pause.

Applying zero seconds to basketball

As we've explained earlier, the zero seconds concept starts with being prepared to shoot upon catching the ball. But what are the other decisions that are available to a player? The zero seconds concept simplifies this into a list of four actions:

1. Shoot – defender backs off, the first decision should be to take the shot.

2. First step – defender is up tight, the next decision should be to attack with the first step.
3. Counter – defender slides to block off the first step, the next decision should be to launch into a counter move.
4. Pass – if a teammate has a better chance to score, pass to them.

Note that this is not a list of priorities – players need to learn how to make the right decision and this is when basketball decision training comes in. The zero seconds concept is about teaching all these skills together, so that players can fluidly switch between one action and the next when making decisions.

Quick summary: players need to do drills that teach multiple fundamentals at once so that they'll be able to apply them in games.

What is basketball decision training and why should I use it?

In simple terms, basketball decision training is about using signals to make drills different with every run through in order to engage a player's decision making. Coach Oliver came up with the concept after being inspired by educational psychologist Dr Joan Vicker's research theory of decision training and her book, Perception, Cognition, and Decision Training. Dr Vicker's book explains the difference between behavioral training and decision training – behavioral training is where your player keeps repeating the same drill over and over again, and decision training is when you make the player respond to a cue, such as a defender. Research into decision training has shown that behavioral training translates poorly to games while players who learn through random, game-based practices are much better at retaining skills – and if you can handle a short one page science lecture I can explain why.

Essentially, researchers in the early 1990s were shocked to find that under certain practice conditions, athletes learning new skills performed far worse in games than when they were practicing.

These subjects would show rapid improvement when learning the new skills, but as soon as it came to applying it in a game, they would perform worse than expected. The conditions responsible for the decline were what we know as 'block' behavioral training – drilling skills over and over again with the goal of making the skills automatic, including the use of basic to advanced progressions, and providing plenty of technique feedback.

An example of this in a basketball context would be a shooting drill that involved taking 20 shots in a row from the same corner, with the coach giving feedback after each repetition. The solution to reverse the performance drop off was found to be decision training, which involved the use of random cues, reduced feedback, and mixing technique and tactics in explanations, i.e. basketball decision training.

Now that's not to say that behavior training doesn't teach skills – the same research shows that blocked practices improves performance in practice, sometimes at rates quicker than decision training. However, when asked to compete, performance suffers as athletes become affected by the pressures of competition and are unable to replicate their skills. This is the reason why we see so many coaches fall in love with block training drills. Block practice shows rapid improvement over a short period of time but fails to translate to a real game. Unfortunately, the player is often blamed for the poor translation instead of evaluating the method of practice.

What decision training does differently is that it puts what scientists call a 'cognitive effort' on players – i.e. it forces them to use their brain to make decisions. It is the training and development of the decision-making apparatus in the brain that allows players to recall, select, and apply practiced skills under pressure. Coach Oliver has taken Dr Vicker's concept of decision training to form the basis of basketball decision training. As he noted in his interview with us, "for the first three repetitions [of a blocked drill] there's a little thinking but beyond that it's basically useless."

Basketball decision training is about forcing players to make decisions in tough game-like situations. Sure, some performances in practice might look ugly but overcoming it in drills leads to in-game benefits, including:

- Your players making better decisions in play.
- Better long-term retention of critical skills.
- Players learn to appreciate the tactical reasons for their actions.
- Players like practice more as it involves additional competition and engagement.

Quick summary: there's a lot of science to back up decision training – players need to be using their brains as well as their bodies when training.

Applying zero seconds and basketball decision training to drills

Adding decision cues

Having spent so much time talking about theory, it's easier to show you what Coach Oliver means when he's talking about a drill that embodies his zero seconds concept and basketball decision training theories. Take shooting for example – in classic block shooting drills you have two players – one shooter and one passer taking 10 shots each. But how often do you shoot from the same spot 10 times in a row? The answer is basically never. Both players switch off mentally, and this is when you see the shooter and passer 'go through the motions.'

Using basketball decision training, Coach Oliver says you can make the same 'two balls, one shooter' drill more game-like by adding decision cues. The basketball decision training shooting signals are:

- Hands up – pass back.
- Hands down – shoot.
- Step toward shooter – drive.
- Jump to the side – drive and counter.
- Hands out and step toward – pass and cut.
- Hands out on drive – penetrate and kick.

Coach Oliver designed these signals himself to simulate the ones that a player will see in a game. As you can see, each cue is very simple and teaches the main focuses of his offense, i.e. driving and cutting for his motion offense. You can easily incorporate basketball decision training cues into your current drills by thinking about how the drill is meant to tie into your current offense and adding new cues accordingly.

Quick summary: basketball decision training cues are formed by thinking about what options are available to your players in a situation and creating cues to have them respond to it.

Embrace small-sided games to teach team skills

When teaching team skills, Coach Oliver will never run through five-on-zero shell drills or five-man weaves. Instead, he runs through four-on-four and five-on-five small-sided games with his college team. If they're working on wing ball screens, he'll just start the four-on-four in that situation and teach out of the game. As a coach, you need to be prepared to stop games to step in and teach. The hardest part of stopping a game as a novice coach can be learning how to quickly and effectively convey the message to your players. They won't be able to absorb too much information each time, and speaking for too long takes away from time they could use to figure things out. Coach Oliver has very specific 'coaching interventions' that can help you know when and what you're stepping in for:

'Recreate' is when you step in to recreate a situation that you just saw. The question to start with here is 'what could you have done better in this situation?'

'Remind' is when you remind players about a concept they know and should have executed but didn't. The question to start with could be 'what are we focusing on today in practice?'

'Demonstrate' is when you demonstrate what players are doing well or showing them what they need to improve. You can ask them 'why should we be doing this?'

'Foul' is when you step in after a foul to point it out to your players. This can happen a lot with younger players who are picking up the game. The question to ask is 'why did I call a foul?'

One last thing – when stepping in with coaching interventions, always lead with questions and not answers. Coach Oliver points out that questions drive thinking, whereas answers lead to an end. Only by asking questions will your players avoid making the same mistakes.

Quick summary: step into small-sided games with a purpose and always lead with a question.

Teach skills one-on-one in individual training

Returning to the earlier explanation of the zero seconds concept, players need the skills to shoot, pass, and dribble to be able to execute a decision. Every player must first learn to shoot off the catch and how to pass, then develop a quick first step, and then a counter move after that step. When applying this to your own player development program, the key is to think of shooting, dribbling, and passing as a singular set of offensive skills and train them in combination with one another. Your players will never be in a game situation where they'll be asked 'just' to shoot, so individual drills where they aren't switching between skills are a waste of time. The best way to teach players to make these decisions while training fundamentals is to have them pair up with a partner to do individual training work.

Coach Oliver always integrates two or more offensive skills in ways that challenges players both mentally and physically.

One example of this is his 'three dribbles backward' series, in which players take three dribbles backward and then launch into a shot, first step move, or counter move. The purpose of the three dribbles is to add some ball-handling skills into the drill and also teach players to shift their momentum and footwork from going backward to attacking the basket. Initially, players practice these skills individually, then basketball decision training is added as they respond to a cue from a partner. Finally, players can take these skills into a one-on-one or a larger small-sided game. The ultimate goal of an individual training drill is to teach skills that can be applied against a defender, which is something you should always keep in mind.

Quick summary: building up to a one-on-one or team drill is the best way to approach drills for individual training. If they don't teach your players skills to use in either game, they may not be very useful!

Basketball decision training approach to practice planning

How to organize focuses

Coach Oliver says he always starts with what to practice and then how. It's important that every drill has a purpose that ties in with the offensive or defensive system you want to run in a game and you understand how this drill contributes toward building that system. I've made this mistake myself where I've used drills just for the sake of it looking great but not tying them into my team's offensive philosophy.

Another point is spending proportional amounts of time on things that happen in a game. For example, if you're spending 80 percent of your time on sideline out-of-bounds play from the baseline then you have to think about how often that happens in a game. It's probably less than five percent of the time. Keep the focus on either individual one-on-one drills for training fundamentals, or small-sided games with the focus on particular team concepts.

Quick summary: each drill needs a focus and should contribute to your overall plan.

Small ways to maximize your practice efficiency

It's impossible to sum up all the things an elite college coach like Chris Oliver does in practice, but here is a collection of small tips he gave us to help you maximize your time:

1. **More balls, more time on task** – how much time are your players actually spending physically playing basketball? There's a lot of wasted time in most practices. There's players standing around waiting, cooling down, transitioning from drill to drill, and in the end a player might just touch the ball six times in 30 minutes. Make sure you get a ball in each player's hand as much as possible and get everyone involved at all times.

2. **Don't end on the same time each practice** – Coach Oliver also challenges coaches to mix up their practice times. If practice time is fixed, it'll be easier for players to be clock-watchers and that's not what we want. As a coach, your job is to make your players uncomfortable and have them grow from that experience.

3. **Coach from the best down** – often, it's the worst players that get coached the most at the majority of practices. Instead, Coach Oliver asks himself what his best players need to improve and gives drills and feedback to that level. He argues that if you drill to the lowest level your top players will not be challenged, whereas if you coach to the top then everyone will be challenged. If his players need individual work then he'll spend more time with them after practice.

4. **Condition players off the court** – when you're planning to put your players through conditioning drills, take them outside of the gym. Coach Oliver's reasoning behind this is that he wants his basketball court used as a place to focus on basketball only. Other places to practice are the gym room, the track, or even in a corridor.

Quick summary: these are just some small things to make your practices more efficient, but remember it's the little things that make good teams great!

Coaching younger players with basketball decision training and zero seconds

Young kids are notoriously not good at shooting (for reasons beyond their control, as seen by Bob Bigelow's post on page 12)

or making decisions. Can they still be taught with basketball decision training and zero seconds drills? Coach Oliver's answer to this is a resounding yes! The fundamental idea of the zero seconds concept – the need to quickly switch between multiple fundamentals – is still important and should be taught. The basketball decision training approach is a great way for developing complete young players as well as teaching basic basketball tactics to them. However, here are some minor adjustments you should make:

1. **The primary option is now to attack the closeout** – we spent a lot of time explaining how players should catch the ball and be prepared to shoot. For younger players, the same fundamental idea still applies – players need to be prepared to attack the defense rather than just passively give the ball up. This involves using a first step to drive for a closer shot or a pass.

2. **Continue to teach shot preparation** – Coach Oliver still feels that players should catch the ball and be prepared to shoot, rather than being prepared to pass. Even if young players can't actually take that shot, being ready to shoot has their footwork and balance in a better position than being ready to pass. Being ready to shoot also promotes an aggressive mindset, and that is what coaches want.

3. **Focus on footwork, passing, finishing, and dribbling** – there are plenty of other fundamentals beside shooting. Young players can be working on these skills in conjunction with one another so that by the time they become strong enough to actually take jumpers, they've already developed a solid driving

game.

4. **Sometimes block drills are necessary** – Coach Oliver concedes that for players just learning to play the game, block drills are a necessity. Basketball decision training can be quite confusing and players will be unable to mix skills if they haven't practiced one enough. However, he encourages coaches to try to get them to take that switch from block to random practice as soon as possible. Young players learn quicker when challenged than when given something easy to try, and you'll often be surprised with what you get.

Quick summary: with just a few changes in focus, basketball decision training and the zero seconds concept are still very much applicable to younger players.

One last word – you need to get your team to buy into the idea of random practice. It takes a leap of faith to try this unorthodox method and you'll need to sell it to your players and the administration. It'll occasionally look chaotic and sometimes you'll feel like no progress is being made. It's easy to feel good if you take 10 shots from the same spot, but in the end you have to believe in the science and that in the long-term your players will benefit from it.

Overall summary

- Motion offenses require players to make decisions and coaches to design practices that revolve around teaching players how to make them.
- The zero seconds concept is the idea that players need to

make a decision as soon as they catch the ball. Practically, it involves the teaching of multiple fundamentals at once to give players the skills to make these quick decisions.

- The teaching of a 'prepare to shoot' mindset is also part of the zero seconds concept.
- Basketball decision training is developed from Dr Joan Vicker's book Perception, Cognition, and Decision Training: the Quiet Eye in Action and calls for more random, game-based training.
- Adding decision cues, focusing on small-sided games with cued interventions, and running skills in conjunction with one another are practical ways to add basketball decision training and zero seconds concepts to your drills.
- Make sure each drill you have has a focus and contributes to your overall offense or defense.
- Younger kids can still learn basketball decision training and zero second drills, you just need to shift the focus a little from shooting to teaching other fundamentals.
- Players may find this method of training challenging and messy, but it will ultimately have them performing better in games.

5

Attack and counter

"How many points do you get from passing the ball? What about dribbling it?"
– Don Kelbick

Coach Kelbick is a contrarian and has several very unique views on player development:

- He doesn't believe in choices on offense, he believes in giving players a map to follow.
- He doesn't believe players should focus on their weaknesses. Instead, they should work on what they're best at.
- You shouldn't read the defense and let it dictate where to go, you should force your defense to stop you and until they do, keep repeating it.

"If you want your players to succeed you should get them to do what they do best, in practice and in games, and attack with it again and again."

– *Don Kelbick*

Be it the NBA, college, international leagues, or high school, Coach Kelbick has found working on a player's strength to be the formula to successful player development, as opposed to working on their weaknesses. Unfortunately, players and coaches who try to form a player development strategy often focus on weaknesses. This is a problem that starts with an inability to prioritize, to single out the most fundamental strengths of each individual's game, and too much ancillary work.

Coach Kelbick shares a metaphor in a story about rocks and sand:

A company was advertising an opening for a job. Applicants had to come in, fill out some paperwork, and take a test. The test was simple. They were given an empty jar, a handful of rocks, and a bag of sand. To pass the test, the applicant had to simply put everything into the jar. They had an hour to complete the task.

Person after person would attempt it and fail. The studied shapes and weight, measured the jar, worked at the task for the full hour, but no one could complete the task.

Then, a young boy asked if he could try. After their experiences, no one believed he could succeed. If they couldn't do it with all of their education and reasoning, how could a young boy hope to achieve it?

The boy went into the testing room, came out in two minutes, and announced, "I'm done!" Not only had he completed the task, he had room left in the bottle and time to spare. All the other people jumped up in amazement, screaming, "You must be a genius. How did you do it?" The boy answered, simply, "I put the big rocks in first."

By putting the big rocks in first, everything else found its place. Smaller rocks would settle in the gaps where they could fit, and then he poured in the sand. The sand not only filled the jar, but it filled in all the openings, the little crevices, flowed around and under the larger rocks. The sand filled every available space in the jar, such that there was room left on top.

The big rocks serve as an apt metaphor for the fundamentals of basketball – dribbling, shooting, passing – that must fall into place before the sand can settle. As a player, are you really going to work on a step-back three-pointer when you can't make a face up wide-open 18 footer (5.4 m)? Are you really going to work on a John Wall 360-degree layup when you can't make a layup with your weak hand? Are you really going to try to beat someone with a Steph Curry same-hand through-the-legs dribble when you can't dribble with your left hand (or indeed right if you are left-handed)?

It should be clear to you by now that Coach Kelbick has a very specific idea of what fundamentals players should learn, and also a clear strategy for how to select and develop a specialized skill in a player. This has come from over 35 years of coaching experience, including stints as a top division I assistant, head high school coach, and most recently as an individual player development coach for NBA players such as Raja Bell, Carlos Arroyo, Joe Johnson, J.J. Barea. Understandably, I was excited to interview him and our exclusive interview with Coach Kelbick was nothing short of a unique insight into the mind of a basketball lifer.

Quick summary: what are your current 'big rocks'? Do you think that they are truly fundamental to the game?

The big rocks – what to coach in individual player development workouts

We spend so much time thinking about how to coach skills that we don't pause to think whether what we're coaching is going to contribute to a player's development. Don't believe me? Just take a look at the vast number of YouTube channels and coaching clinics demonstrating different methods to teach skills, and compare it to how few in-depth discussions we coaches have about what skills we should be teaching in the first place. On the other hand, shooting, passing, defense, dribbling, etc. are all taken for granted as 'the fundamentals' and are expected to be taught to everybody to the same level.

In my conversation with Coach Kelbick, I realized just how wrong I was to approach individual player development with such a fixed mindset. I'd always thought that individual player development workouts were about working on weaknesses or molding a player to a position. In fact, these ideas are the exact opposite of what Coach Kelbick argues for. He told me that to succeed at any level of basketball you need to specialize, and that means focusing on an individual's strengths and coaching them to the highest level possible.

We covered three major themes across our discussion:

- To coach strengths or to coach weaknesses.
- To coach for the player or to coach for the position.
- To coach one skill or many.

It may sound controversial, but your current approach to player development may be wrong. Let's see if I can convince you to put the 'individual' back into individual player development.

Big rock 1: coach strengths over weaknesses

Based on my personal experience, I believe this is the number one mistake coaches make when forming player development sessions. We've all heard stories about players who stay back after practice to work with the coach on a weakness. Perhaps it is because of our instincts as coaches to always seek flaws in our player's games that we feel compelled to focus on these areas. However, from his many years of coaching, Don Kelbick provided a compelling argument as to why coaches shouldn't make coaching weaknesses the key emphasis of individual training plans.

Coach Kelbick noted that it is very, very rare for a weakness to ever become a point of strength. In part this can be explained by the rule of diminishing returns, which means that the more hours you spend on teaching a skill, the harder it becomes to get better at it. The reality is that true all-round players are once-in-a-generation talents (see LeBron James for example). The rest of us have to learn to specialize. But if you could train someone to do one thing on the court as great as LeBron James does, I'd argue that they would have a place on any high school or college team.

Payers with outstanding strengths are often what win teams games, but basketball is still a team game – meaning that your players don't have to be able to do everything on their own. Great coaches come in and are able to put players into a position where they can utilize their best skills to succeed. Likewise, skilled coaches should be able to cover up for a player's weaknesses on both ends of the floor.

Learning to focus on strengths is particularly valid for middle and high school players who have much less time than college or professional players to practice one-on-one with a coach. Coach Kelbick would say that school teams are better off working on a weakness up to a point where it doesn't become a net minus for a team (ideally in team practices) and using individual training time to focus on strengths.

Big rock 2: coach the player, not the position

Coach Kelbick is a believer in coaching for the individual rather than the position. He told Coachbase this: "I've always believed that the essence of coaching is not for me to get you to do what I want you to do. The essence of coaching is for me to get you to do what it is that you do best, to the best of your ability." You might see high school, AAU, and sometimes even middle-school coaches wanting to impose their own system and philosophy on their players. The problem with this rigid way of thinking is that it is essentially a process of trying to fix square pegs into round holes. Even if it yields success for the team, at the individual level players are essentially learning a role for that system rather than being asked to improve their own skill set. All great coaches have a knack of being able to adapt their system to their roster.

Big rock 3: coach one skill over many

Coach Kelbick uses a quote from the great Jerry West to illustrate this point: "There are no extraordinary players. There are only ordinary players that do one or two things extraordinarily well." Young players sometimes feel the pressure to be good at many skills, or they may not even know what skills they are good at. Coach Kelbick always makes the effort to praise players during drills to highlight the areas of the game they excel at. Phrases like "you're the best on this team at X skill", or "if you keeping working hard at X you could be a very special player" make a big difference whether he's coaching an NBA-level player or a middle school kid at one of his many coaching clinics, and the benefits are apparent across the board. Players become more confident on attack, and coaches know that they can rely on that player to perform their role well.

Quick summary: coaching for strengths over weaknesses, player over position, and one skill over many are the criteria for a specialized player approach.

The little rocks - teaching the Attack and Counter mentality

Coach Kelbick believes that an individual workout is more than just teaching skills, it's about teaching an attack mentality for the game. Players need to go into each repetition of a drill being prepared to get the ball into the basket. As such, he's a big fan of taking game shots in practice. These ideas are part of his own philosophy called 'Attack and Counter' which has two key parts to it – 'Attack', which is the first and best move a player has; and 'Counter', the second counter move to exploit the defense if that attack is blocked. I break it down below.

Shoot first mentality

Don Kelbick is staunchly against the traditional 'triple threat' stance and it's 'read and react' mentality. "How many points do you get from passing the basketball? What about dribbling it?" he asked us rhetorically in the interview. Instead of thinking about passing, he tells his players that their mentality should be "think shot! – shooting is 'A' in my basketball alphabet."

The reason why shooting is so fundamental to his 'Attack and Counter' philosophy is that it simplifies the game for his players. Coach Kelbick raises the example of coaches who get mad at players for being indecisive on offense: "Well, that's what you've taught them to do," he says. "You've given him too many options and he's going through his basketball database trying to figure out what's the best one. I have one option in my database: shoot." Coach Kelbick believes that a lot of coaches make the game too complex and that leads to 'analysis paralysis' in a game. He's a proponent of leaving your brain at the door by giving each player a map of moves to follow. Here's how it works:

- Immediately use a go-to move on the catch.
- If defense stops the move, use counter move A.
- If counter move A is stopped, use counter move B.

By eliminating decisions and having a trusted map of skills that players have practiced, it gives them confidence and allows them to be more aggressive. That's why the first option is always to look to shoot. By being in a shooting stance on catching the ball, their footwork and balance gets better, and they're able to pass or drive. In addition, because they're looking at the rim their head is up and they can see the full court.

The 'shoot first' mentality applies whether your players are specialized in scoring from the low post, perimeter, or midrange. If your players are catching the ball in places they can't shoot from, then you need to move them to places where they can be a threat to the defense from the moment they catch the ball. Here is where big rock number 2, 'coach the player, not the position' applies. There is nothing wrong with a guard being most effective from the low block or a forward from the perimeter. If they are most accurate shooting from there, this is the spot where you should run your individual drills from.

Quick summary: catching the ball with the intention to shoot gets your body and mind in the best position to score.

Teach counters in a progression and emphasize footwork

After perfecting the core move, the jump shot, Coach Kelbick teaches counters so that players can attack when the defense defends the first option well. Looking at the sets of drills he gave us, there is a logical progression to the series of counters he teaches:

1. Give and go backdoor cut.

2. Shot fake drive middle.
3. First step drive.
4. Crossover step drive.
5. Drive middle with spin move.
6. One-dribble crossover.
7. One-dribble double crossover.

How many of you would have guessed that the first counter to the shot is the backdoor cut? Often players think that it's the crossover, but as you can see it's sixth on our list. That's because Coach Kelbick's philosophy is that players prioritize footwork in counters. If the first option – shooting – is a threat, defenders have to guard the player closely, leaving them off balance and vulnerable to being beaten by cuts, shot fakes, a quick first step, or crossover steps. One unique insight he gave us about cutting was that players need to be ready to 'attack' even without the ball. He explains: "Attacking is a mentality – it's about forcing the defender to do something that he doesn't want to do." The cut is the perfect first counter to the shot because it relies on taking what the defense gives you rather than playing into something that is well guarded.

Moreover, footwork is actually easier to teach and more effective than dribble moves at beating players. It can take thousands of hours of practice to learn to crossover with the quickness, efficiency, and balance needed to get past a player, but an ankle breaker gets you exactly zero points in a game. It is better to spend that time on developing an accurate shot and quick feet to get easier shots.

Quick summary: the easiest and most effective counters are those that focus on footwork. Have your players master them before getting fancy with dribble moves.

The sand - how to teach skills

So now that I've explained Coach Kelbick's philosophies, it is time to get into the specifics as to how he runs his individual practice plans. You can see a sample plan on page 266.

Take game shots

Coach Kelbick knows where his players are best at scoring from before a practice session starts and so he sets up shop in that area of the court. Every one of the shots taken in practice are expected to be the same type a player would make in a game. Common areas where players score from in games are the low block, elbows, perimeter wings, corners, and at the top.

Use fewer drills, run higher repetitions

Unlike many coaches, Coach Kelbick only uses four or five different drills for an entire hour's workout. This reinforces his philosophy by allowing players to repeatedly do what they do best. In fact, they get to do what they do best a lot in one session – Coach Kelbick aims to run as many as 300–400 shots in an hour's session.

Work around the jump shot and take your time through the progressions

Don Kelbick is able to run so many repetitions by keeping the drills simple. Each workout is just a progression – after practicing the jump shot from that area, they then move onto give and go. There is no rush to move through the entire progression in one session; rather, the focus is to make sure that counter is mastered.

Keep workouts short

Don Kelbick's workouts with NBA players only ever last between an hour to an hour and 15 minutes. The reasons he outlined for us were both mental and physiological. Mentally, he says, the short period of each workout helps players practice with a higher effort and intensity. Physiologically, packing in a high number of similar repetitions in a short amount of time trains muscle memory, helping players to transfer their skills to a game.

Demand high effort

"The one thing that sets NBA players apart from the rest is their effort", says Coach Kelbick, "they may get exhausted, but when it's time to work – they work. Their capacity for work is so far beyond other players that it's staggering." Remind your own players of this point. Regardless of what skill level your players are at, they must be prepared to give 100 percent to each of your sessions if they want to improve. You are taking time out of your schedule to help them practice one-on-one and so they must be equally as committed.

Quick summary: an intense one-hour workout is ideal for teaching individual skills.

A fitting final insight that Coach Kelbick gave us was how he views coaching players and, more broadly, life. He summarizes his sentiments as follows: "people rarely do things for you, but they'll do things in spite of what you want." Rather, to get people to change Coach Kelbick says, "The role of a coach is to convince a player to believe that the change the coach thinks that he should make is the best thing for him to succeed." In other words, the will to change has to come from the player rather than from an external force. However, this requires a high level of trust between the player and coach that they both genuinely want to improve the player's game.

Coach Kelbick illustrates how this trust is formed with a point NBA coach Mike D'Antoni made to him about his player-coach relationship with Steve Nash. Coach D'Antoni could never even imagine shouting at Steve Nash, Coach Kelbick says, because they both believe that they're working toward the same goal: helping Steve to be a better player. This may seem like a simple message but it can be so easy to get frustrated in pressure situations, never mind the intensity of an NBA game.

What I take away from this is that coaches need to take a patient approach when working individually with players. There is only so much that you can show them. It can seem like you're putting in a lot of effort for very little results, but all it takes is one moment of success and you will have a player believing in your intentions and your methods.

Overall summary

- Individual player specialization is the key to success at all levels of basketball and should frame how you run your solo workouts.
- Always make sure that your big rocks are set before you lay down the little rocks and sand.
- The big rocks – ensuring that you are coaching for strengths over weakness, player over position, and one skill over many will keep you focused on specialization.
- The little rocks – preparing an 'Attack and Counter' mentality starts with 1. The intention to shoot. 2. Prioritizing footwork to teach counters.
- The sand – short workouts of high intensity are best.
- Think about this: the role of a coach is to convince a player to believe that the change the coach thinks that he should make is the best thing for him to succeed. Do you agree?

6

How to develop the next Steve Nash

My father was a soccer player. All my friends played basketball though, so I stuck with basketball- Steve Nash

If you saw Steve Nash when he was a child, you'd never have guessed that he'd grow up to become the NBA legend he is today. The two times MVP had just started playing basketball in eighth grade. Soccer was his main sport, but he also played hockey, lacrosse, and rugby. To the basketball coaches that see a like-minded young player experiment with three or four different sports and worry about a lack of 'commitment' or 'dedication', Ron Yeung, manager of Canada Basketball's Youth Development Program has a message for you: "experimenting is okay, it's normal, and in fact it's better for their development as an athlete in the long term."

Ron Yeung had some great insights for Coachbase as he talked about his experience of developing Canada's Long-Term Athlete Development (LTAD) program. With a population of only 35 million as opposed to the United States' 319 million,

Canada Basketball's youth program has had a much smaller talent pool to draw from. In addition, basketball faces tough competition from other popular sports such as ice hockey, lacrosse, rugby, soccer, and baseball. With these factors in mind, Canada Basketball teamed up with sports scientists and researchers to develop the LTAD. Rather than trying to compete, Canada Basketball encourages its young players to build up vital motor and decision-making skills by playing other sports. Moreover, the recently launched Steve Nash Youth Basketball program has given thousands of youth coaches the training and resources they need to coach basketball. If you coach an elementary or middle school team, these are our four principles that you can apply to create your own youth basketball program that will have your kids loving the game for life!

Realize that movement skills are the true fundamentals

In his interview with Coachbase, Ron Yeung stated that he views his young players as "athletes first, basketball players second." While this may sound strange to the basketball coach, take as an example a young player who is having difficulty learning the one-two rhythm of a layup. On the court, the problem might be that the player is traveling often or frequently clanging layups off the backboard. The more fundamental weakness, however, might be that the player struggles with skipping, a basic movement skill.

Canada Basketball calls these movement skills 'physical literacy' – the ability of a young child to 'move confidently and with control' and also read and react to activities going on around them. The extent of a child's activity from the ages of 0–12 during the most rapid stages of development of the nervous system plays a key role in determining their physical literacy later on in life. Fortunately, most kids naturally enjoy being active! It's up to you, the coach, to have them play fun games that will build a variety of different movement skills.

Build movement skills through multiple sports

To help youth coaches figure out what sports contribute to developing fundamental movement skills, Canada Basketball designed the table below.

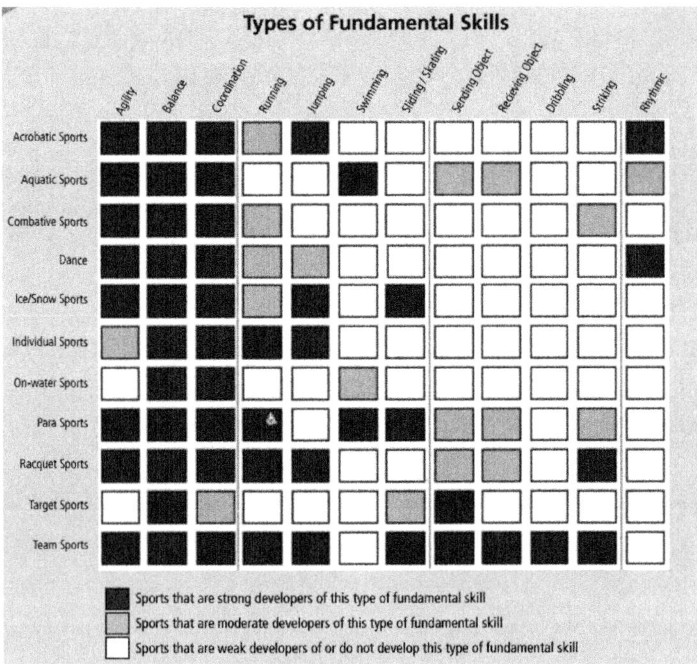

Source: Basketball Canada

Using Steve Nash as example, Ron Yeung explained how his participation in many sports, particularly soccer, influenced and helped make him a great basketball player: "You can see that there are many skills that transferred from soccer – for example when you see him on the court, his footwork is just amazing. Different skills that you use from different sports allow you to transfer those skills and get better at it." As for the coaches worried about a lack of focus: "Kids will narrow down their sports in junior high to two sports that they're really good at", he says, "but for the elementary school age, let them have fun, let them play and try as many sports as possible." We suggest that you take his advice.

Apply the principles of fun, age appropriateness, and progressions when selecting drills. These three principles are vital for developing skills in young players and motivating them to stay in the game. Unfortunately, coaches often forget about them when they opt to run a layup line for 200 makes. Here's what Ron had to say about each:

1. **Fun** – "First and foremost you want to make sure that your kids are having fun and enjoying the sport." Fun should be your first criteria if you're selecting a drill for an elementary school team.
2. **Age appropriateness** – have your players developed the necessary motor and basketball skills to run the drill?
3. **Progressions** – "Before we even get too specialized into basketball we need to make sure the kids have developed a base of motor skills. After that, we want to develop global players." 'Global players' is a term Canada Basketball uses to describe all-rounded players that have worked on all

the skills and trained to play in every position. As a coach, you need to understand why it's important that even big players learn how to handle the ball and smaller ones learn to rebound, and how to make a drill more or less difficult depending on the stage of a player's development (hint: find the answers in the resources below).

Think outside of the box to get inspiration for drills

Surprisingly, Ron said that one of the main groups that Canada Basketball works with are P.E. teachers. Although these teachers don't specialize in any sport, they've often got an extensive knowledge of games that kids love and can learn motor skills from. Often, these drills are then easily modified to make them more basketball specific. If you haven't already, ask the P.E. teachers at your school for advice!

These are the four principles we learned from Ron Yeung that help Canada Basketball's Long-Term Athlete Development Program consistently produce elite talent. If you're an elementary coach who's just starting out, or even an experienced veteran, there are plenty of insights in here that you can apply to your own program. Coaching an elementary school team is never easy but the rewards are worth it when you can spread the love of the game to other young players.

Beanbag drill

If there's a magic drill that's also extremely fun then it's this one. You can use beanbags, pinnies, or cones to play the beanbag game. We recommend that you read through the entire article, but if you want you can watch the video to understand the basic concepts, then feel free to skip forward to the level or age group that your team is at:

- Beginner progressions (for U6 teams)
- Intermediate progressions (for U11 teams)
- Advanced progressions (for U16 teams)

The great thing about the beanbag drills are they are all part of one progression. Once you've learned the basic concepts, we demonstrate that it's very easy to adjust the difficulty of the drill to teach more advanced basketball concepts to your players.

Progression 1

In the first part of the game, the beanbags are all in the center of the court. You can have up to three players per team go at a time. The child scores a basket and runs to the center to retrieve a beanbag, then places the beanbag in the team's hula hoop. The next child in line then has a go. The kids keep scoring baskets until all of the beanbags are depleted from the middle. The coach can determine how many children can go at a time, but it is best to allow only two or three children from each group to go at any given time. Record which teams have the greatest number of beanbags.

In the second part of the game, the players must now run to the far end and shoot a basket. After making the basket, the players take a beanbag from the opposing team's hula hoop, return it to their own end, and place the captured beanbag in their team's hula hoop. Restrict the number of players who go at any one time.

Time the length of the game, and count which team has the most beanbags in order to determine the winner. If time permits, repeat the second phase. This time, though, add a restricted area from which the ball must be shot behind. A skipping rope is a good way to mark this space.

Progression 2

In progression 2, dribbling is added to the game. The players make their shot, rebound the ball, and dribble to center court to collect the beanbag if they made the basket. Encourage the players to alternate which hand they dribble with. This part of the game is played until all the beanbags are gone from the center.

In the second part of this game, the players now have to dribble the length of the floor to shoot the ball. If they are successful, collect the beanbag and dribble back.

The third part is to tell players that they must shoot the ball from outside the key.

Time the length of the game, and count which team has the most beanbags in order to determine the winner.

Progression 3

In this progression, the concept of changing directions and changing hands is added. The players must now dribble through cones or pylons before retrieving the beanbag. There are two options on how to proceed:

a) The players can dribble and carry the beanbag at the same time (one method is to place it on their head), or:
b) The coach can keep track at center court by placing the beanbags in a team's hoop when the task has been successfully completed.

Now the players must dribble through the pylons to the opposite end of the floor, shoot, and retrieve a beanbag.

Again, the players can carry the beanbag back or the coach can keep score.

The final phase is to extend the shooting range with the skipping rope.

Progression 4

In this progression, the concept of protecting the ball while dribbling is added. Each team places a defender inside a hula hoop at the other end of the floor. After the player makes a shot, he/she must dribble between the pylons where the defender is located. If the child loses control of the ball, he/she must retrieve it and return through the pylons. Be sure to change the defender.

The second part is to dribble to the far basket through the stationary defender. The final part is to get players to shoot from outside the key. As you can see, in each session the players play the game three times, with each round becoming progressively more difficult.

Progression 5

In this progression, we have added multiple stationary defenders. The defenders stand inside the hula hoops to restrict their movement. Be sure to change the directions the teams travel and also the defenders.

There are still the same three progressions:

a) Shoot at the near basket, dribble to half and back.

b) Dribble to the far basket, shoot, and dribble back – this promotes using layups.

c) Add the key restriction rule – this promotes shooting from further out.

Remember to allow the children to rebound and make their shot.

Progression 6

In this progression, an active defender is added. You should remind the defense that they want to put their body between the offensive player and the basket. Hitting or slapping is not allowed. The players must dribble through a designated area in which the defender is allowed to play. Be sure to switch the sides of the floor and the defenders.

There are still the three progressions:
a) Shoot, go to half, and then back to your own end.
b) Go to the other end to score.
c) Add a key.

Progression 7

This progression has multiple active defenders, and the dribbler must navigate his/her way through the three defensive zones. Be sure to mix up the direction the players dribble and the defenders.

Still use your three progressions:
a) To the halfway line.
b) To the far end.
c) Add the key restriction rule.

Progression 8

This progression adds the idea of passing the ball. The players work on going in pairs, passing the ball back and forth as they advance. After each player scores a basket, the players return while passing the ball. When returning, one player passes and runs to get in front of the other player. This gives the players two ways of partner passing. Still use the same three progressions. Notice that the coach is on the sideline keeping score with the beanbags.

Remember to use your three progressions:
a) To the halfway line.
b) To the far end.

c) Add the key restriction rule.

Progression 9

Now, static defenders are added to the passing. The defensive players must stay inside the hoops. On the way down the floor, the players pass while running side-by-side. On the way back, one player passes and runs to get in front of the player to whom he/she just passed. Be sure to mix up the defenders and the sides of the floor the players move down and back.

Remember to use the same three progressions:
a) Score at your own end.
b) Score at the far end with layups.
c) Score at the far end with shots.

Notice that the coach is again on the sideline keeping score with the beanbags.

There are still the three progressions:
a) Shoot – go to half and back to your own end.
b) Go to the other end to score.
c) Add the key restriction rule.

Progression 10

The final progression is to have active defenders in three zones that the offensive players must pass around and over. Be sure to mix up the defenders. Some of the children may have to be reminded about what is allowed on defense.

Still use the same three progressions:
a) Score at your own end.
b) Score at the far end with layups.
c) Score at the far end with shots.

Notice that the coach is on the sideline keeping score with the beanbags.

Your players have now learned the basic concepts of the game of basketball.

There are still the three progressions:
a) Shoot go to half and back to your own end.
b) Go to the other end to score.
c) Add the key restriction rule.

7

Developing players with flair the Spanish way

Do you ever watch players like Ricky Rubio and wonder where they get their creativity and flair from? If you watched him training at FC Barcelona, you'll realize that those amazing passes he throws today aren't accidents – he practiced those 'behind the back no look passes' from a young age.

Coach Joe Riley spent many years in Spain learning about how the Spanish train their youth and in this interview he'll share:

- Why he's never seen a single shell drill in Spain.
- How to create players with 'flair' or their own identity as opposed to every player playing exactly the same way.
- Why should you teach step away three-point runners and behind the back passes to 13-year-olds?
- How the coaches in Spain don't have a set drill book. They create new drills every practice.
- Where to draw inspiration for new drill ideas.

Coach Riley spent many years coaching youth basketball at Club Estudiantes in Madrid. Estudiantes developed five of the 12 players who eventually won Spain's only basketball World Championship in 2006, including Spanish legends Sergio Rodriguez, Carlos Jimenez, and Felipe Reyes, cementing their reputation for developing young players.

Coach Riley said the thing that blew his mind when he sat in on their practices was the atmosphere. Instead of 'sprint, sprint, sprint' and 'you have to do this, you have to do that, it has to be perfect', there was a lot of freedom and practice was much more relaxed and fun! Coming from the United States' more 'traditional' coaching background where the focus was on drilling in a lot of offensive plays that require perfect execution and high intensity, it was a breath of fresh air.

What makes the Spanish practice structure special?
Does this look like an outline of your practice plan?

1. Three-man weave.
2. Three v two into two v one.
3. Shell drill.
4. Five v five.

"You could do that everyday and you could get good, but is that good enough?"
– Joe Riley

Coach Riley explained his comments from his time observing Club Estudiantes, where instead of building up a skill from basic to advanced progressions, they let players try the drill with a lot of repetitions and then get them to use it in a small-sided game. For example, when teaching a crossover the coach would demonstrate 10 variations and have the players pick three they liked. That way, each player can work on mastering those three to build their own unique identity.

This is what a practice would look like:

One v zero ball spike. Use any finish you like (nine minutes).

Three v three small-sided games. Use as many ball spikes as possible (nine minutes).

One-dribble pull-up (nine minutes).

The first minute of each drill is a demonstration of what the skill looks like, followed by eight minutes of high repetition practice. Coaches observe and give individual feedback after the players have attempted the skill themselves.

Creating a fun, relaxed, and encouraging atmosphere

> *"It's not about the execution but more about decision-making."*
> *– Joe Riley*

When Coach Riley (and likely most of you) thinks of practice, you probably conjure up these images:

- A high intensity environment with the coach barking out instructions like "sprint, sprint, SPRINT!"
- Everything has to be perfectly executed. Running set plays to perfection multiple times with the exact same two-handed perfect pass.
- Every player is executing the same drills and plays in the same way.

That's why Coach Riley was blown away by how different it was in Spain. He observed:

- A very relaxed, fun, and free of judgment atmosphere.
- Players being encouraged to try new and different skills. Every player had their own playing style.
- Coaches were very encouraging. They tended to focus on decision-making rather than the execution. Sometimes there was lots of turnovers and balls flying out of bounds but it was encouraged.

Why you should let players try difficult skills and disguise it as fundamental

'Behind the back, no look passes' are also fundamentals. If you don't start at age 10, you won't do it when you're 35-years-old.

First of all, what is a fundamental skill? Surely, a step-away three-point runner is not a fundamental skill for 13-year-olds. Yet, this is exactly what they did at Club Estudiantes. Coach Riley was surprised to see the coaches encouraging full-court one-handed passes off the dribble for 10-year-olds. Nine out of 10 of those passes literally flew off the court.

He asked the coach why they were encouraging this and the coach said "In a real game, would you rather have two slow but safe passes or one risky pass that gets the ball there in one go? By the end of the season, it'll be there." Instead of taking multiple perfect passes to set up a fast break, you'll get a one-handed cross-court pass that sets up the layup instantly. It's all about balancing risk against reward in these situations.

Coach Riley poses this question: if you don't let your players work on their behind the back pass at 10-years-old, why will they learn this skill at the age of 30?

> *"Coaches may say you really can't practice that skill! But you need it! Every skill has its place. If you can't, you're going to struggle. Throw a lot at them from a young age and let them pick."*
> *– Joe Riley*

To Riley, there are many benefits to teaching all skills as fundamentals:

- If you make every skill, including advanced ones like missing step floaters, a fundamental, then your players won't be so afraid to try it and will assume it's necessary to their development.
- If you don't try it at a young age, when will you learn it?
- It makes practice fun. Kids will surprise you and they love a challenge.

Example: how to teach an attack mentality and giving players the skills required.

A lot of turnovers, a lot of mistakes. Perfection is not stressed.

An example of foregoing short-term mistakes for long-term games is by teaching the attack mentality. At Club Estudiantes they emphasized having an attack mentality, meaning you attack as soon as you catch the ball.

Early in the season, you'll see a lot of turnovers but it's only later in the season that you'll start seeing results. It's also not enough to talk about having an attack mentality – you have to give players the skills to do this, such as the ball spike pass.

Usually when you come off a cut on the perimeter, players catch the ball and come to a full jump stop, which slows down speed. The ball spike is a great move that basically means you slap the ball onto the ground as you cut so you can keep moving toward the basket.

How to develop creativity or flair in players

Coach Riley asked one of the coaches if he had a drill book that he picked drills from. "What's a drill book?" was the response. The coaches created new drills every practice and no drill was repeated twice. It's a lot of work but here's the reasoning behind it:

- In order for your players to be creative, you have to be creative as a coach. Lead by example.
- It makes it fun and interesting for the players.
- No practice is the same, it's always new.
- Don't be afraid of mistakes – if a drill doesn't work then cut it short and move on.
- There's always ways to improve. Even if a drill is great, you can always make it better.

How to come up with new drills

It's better to have a mind that is better at creating drills than having a drill book packed with drills. It's difficult to generate ones for every practice but it can be done. As simple as it sounds, Coach Riley says he draws ideas from watching games. That's both professional EuroLeague and amateur youth level games. You can do this too. When you see a skill you like, you can break it down and teach it to your players.

Once you've identified a skill you want to teach, here are some guidelines for using it in practice:

- Keep it simple. If you're working on shooting, you don't need to touch 20 cones and then shoot.
- Don't worry about rotations, the players will figure it out for themselves.
- Strip the skill down to a bare minimum.
- Practice a skill, give it lots of repetitions, and then have your players try it in a small-sided game. There should be no penalties for mistakes.

Sometimes you don't need to think it through completely. You can be intentionally vague. For example: make two teams of three players. Drop two basketballs on the ground – the first team to score wins. Some players will dribble but some will figure out that passing is faster than dribbling. Let the players think through the problems, they might surprise you.

One-on-one as a great way to teach (small-sided games)

Before coming to Spain, Coach Riley struggled with coaching one-on-one so he asked their coaches how do to it. Easy, they said. There are different positions to start a one-on-one:

- Defender in front.
- Defender behind.

- Defender on the hip.

Start with the defender touching the offensive player. On the coach's signal, they go live. If it's too difficult, make the defender hold a ball or put their hands behind their backs. While teaching one-on-one, coach the details. For example, with a defender on the hip you want to:

- Keep the ball as wide as possible.
- Push the ball as forward as possible.
- Stay low.
- Sprint to the basket.
- Extend and reach when finishing.

The Spanish coaches loved using one-on-one as a teaching tool and as a result many of the 10-year-olds were very adapt at scoring and had skills to finish under pressure with a finger roll.

Another concept is to build advantages on top of advantages. This means using skill as opposed to relying on athleticism. You should read your defender and create an advantage based on their feet positioning and orientation.

Summary

At the end of the interview Coach Riley told us that he enjoys basketball that is entertaining, fun, and exciting. If you want to play that way, you should be training that way. If you teach everything as a fundamental, kids will think it's fundamental. If you make it seem advanced, then they will be hesitant to use it. Every skill has a place. Nothing is wrong. Look at decision, not execution.

8

Dell Curry shooting secrets

"The key is not the 'will to win'... everybody has that. It is the will to prepare to win that is important."
– Bob Knight

Dell Curry was one of the most deadly shooters in the NBA when he played for the Charlotte Hornets. He is father to Steph and Seth Curry. Discover his shooting secrets here.

Missing left to right

1 Walk to side of backboard

2 Shoot the ball towards backboard

Missing left to right

Reason: probably the most common mistake is caused by incorrect positioning of the elbows. Make sure the elbows are in line to the basket and not flaring out to the side.

How to fix: find a backboard or a straight line on a wall. Shoot the basketball and try to hit the same spot every time.

Open window

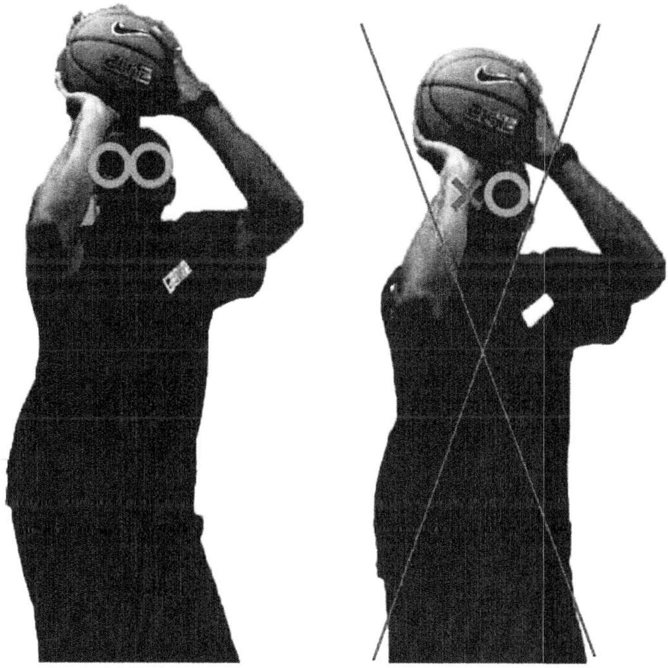

Don't let your arm block your vision, make sure both of your eyes can see the basket.

Drill: find a spot on the wall. Go into your shooting stance, close each eye, and make sure you can still see the dot. Keep repeating the shooting motion and make sure neither arm blocks your view.

Poor extension

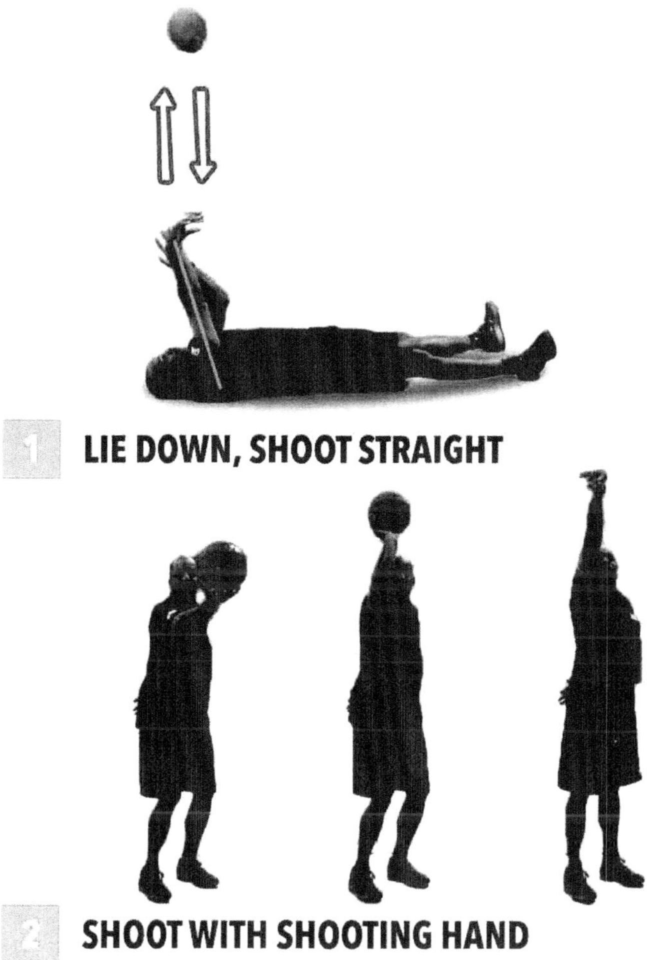

If you don’t follow through and extend all the way at the top of your shot, this drill is for you.

Drill: lie on the ground with ball in hand. Shoot the ball straight up and it should land straight back down. Remember to follow through.

Low point of release

1 **JUMP & THROW** 2 **CATCH & SHOOT**

You want to release the ball as high as you can. If you are shooting from the hip, it is easier to block. Steph Curry use to shoot from his chest but over one summer he worked with his dad to release the ball above his head.

Drill: throw the ball to the backboard and catch the rebound without bringing it back down. Jump twice with the ball high and then shoot. The key is to keep the ball high.

Two thumbs

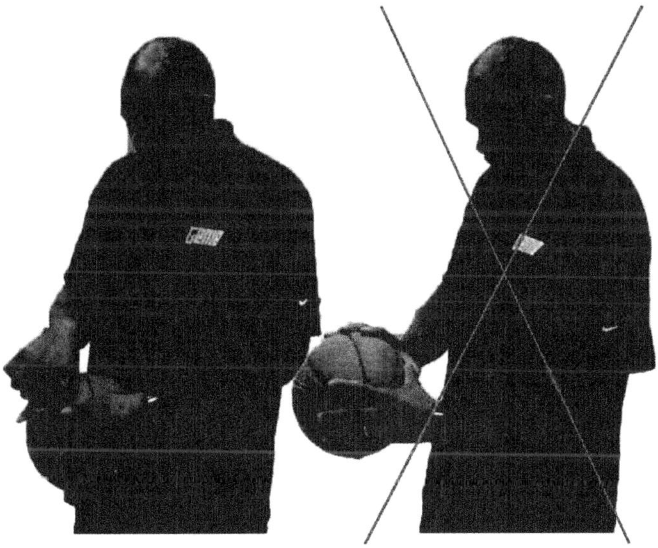

If your guide hand is too involved – meaning both thumbs are on the ball and pointing toward you – then that's a problem. You want your guide thumb to be pointing toward the ceiling when you are in a shooting stance.

Drill: spin the ball and catch it. Make sure your guide hand is on the side and when you go into your stance it's pointing up.

Eliminating dip on shot

1 **DIP BEFORE YOU CATCH THE BALL**

Imagine this scenario: catch the ball, dip (bend your knees), and then shoot. If you are already in the dip position you can catch and shoot. Which is faster? Dell Curry says you should do the work early and already be in a dip position when you catch to have a quicker release.

Drill: spin the ball and catch the ball in dip position.

Drifting

Missing in front or behind the basket is better than missing left or right. On a jump shot, if you land to the left or right of where you started then you're drifting. You want to either stay in the same spot or jump forward slightly.

Drill: mark a spot on the floor and take a shot. Make sure you land on the same spot after every shot.

Guide hand

Guide hand

You want your guide hand to be level with your shooting hand until the point of release. If you leave your guide hand too early then players tend to push the ball or lose control.

Drill: find a mirror and without a basketball go into your shooting motion. At the point of release, pause and check if your guide hand is level with your shooting hand.

9

Dribbling drills

The key to great handles is unsurprising – time spent dribbling. Kyrie Irving, Steph Curry, and James Harden all spend hours each day practising this fundamental skill.

As a coach, it's good to have plenty of drills in your drill library for the following two reasons:

1. To make an otherwise repetitive exercise (such as pounding a ball) fun for your players, especially young kids.
2. Teach and develop certain skills for games.

These are some of the best dribbling drills available in the practice planner and we've arranged them according to:

- Teaching dribbling to kids (U9s).
- Game-based drills (U12s and U14s).
- Team drills (U14s and U16s).
- Solo drills (all age groups).

Teaching dribbling to kids

Dribble, jump stop and pivot right hand, left hand

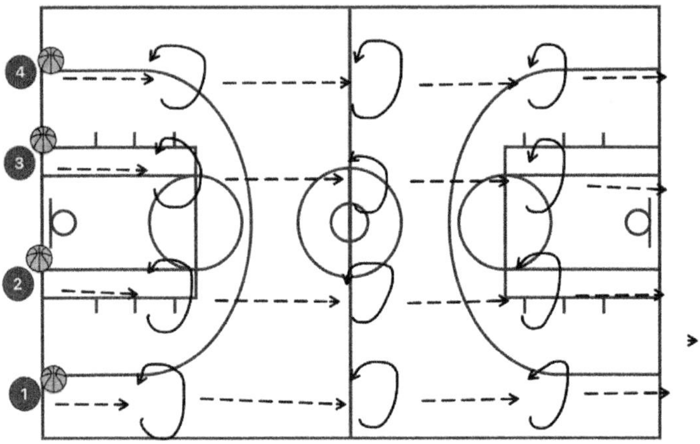

Dribble, jump stop and pivot right hand, left hand

Why it's great

Pivoting after picking up the dribble is a fundamental yet often neglected part of dribbling the ball. Young players who aren't taught this often travel or can't use footwork effectively to get separation when they become older. Bob Bigelow, youth sports coach and former NBA player, loves this drill and teaches it to all age groups, with this being the first progression.

Setup

Players line up along the baseline, spread out, each with a ball.

Instructions

On the coach's whistle, players take two dribbles forward with the right hand and pick the ball up with a jump stop. Then they pivot to the left, back, right, and front again in a full circle, all on the left foot. Reach the end and repeat with the left hand.

Coaching points

- Make sure players have their knees bent when pivoting – this helps them keep their balance and control.
- After picking the ball up with a jump stop, players should hold it at chest height, elbows out protecting the ball.

Wall finger tip drill

Wall finger tip drill

Why it's great

This drill is the equivalent of doing weights – except that all you're working against is gravity! By dribbling against a wall, your kids will be working on their strength so that dribbling on the court will seem much easier.

Setup

Players face a wall with a basketball.

Instructions

Players find a spot on the wall just above their head to try to hit it consistently. Bounce the ball against the wall, trying to keep the ball in place. Run for five minutes and swap hands.

Coaching points

- Once players have mastered accuracy, the key is to master speed. Try to limit holding the ball in hand – as soon as it touches the fingers, dribble again.
- The distance from the wall determines the drill's difficulty. New players should stand up to 3 ft (0.9 m) away. More experienced players can stand right up against it.

Shot fake and pivot drill

Shot fake and pivot drill

Why it's great

A good shot fake should be considered a dribble move – after all it gets the defender out of position in preparation for a drive to the rim. This is another drill to be taught at a young age as it can be effective at all levels.

Setup

Players stand in lines, each with a ball, facing the coach.

Instructions

Players protect the ball, holding it at waist height. At the coach's call, they move their dominant foot forward into a shooting stance, and shot fake. Protect the ball again and repeat.

Coaching points

- Coach Bigelow explains that the shot fake can't be too high – the point is to get the defender, not you, off balance. Keeping the ball low also allows it to be put to the ground quicker for a drive.
- Emphasizing the use of the body to protect the ball is also an important part of this drill. Your players will need to learn to quickly move between protecting the ball, shot faking, and dribbling.

Dribble perimeter

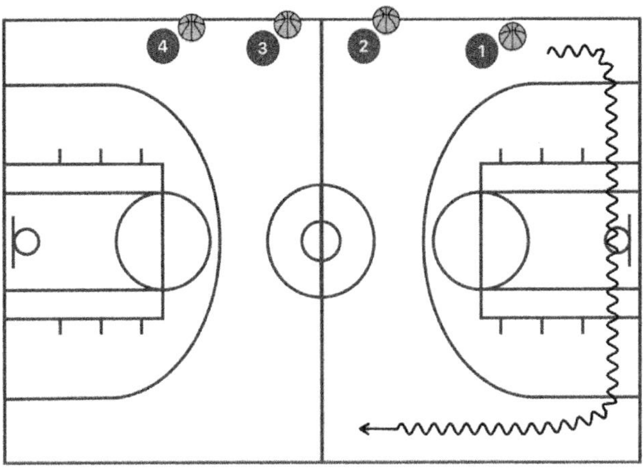

Dribble perimeter

Why it's great

Dribbling and stopping while under control is something even high school players can have trouble with. This is a fundamental skill that needs to be taught at a young age.

Setup

Players line up along the perimeter, each with a ball.

Instructions

Players face the same direction and begin dribbling at a third of max speed. At the first whistle, pick the ball up and pivot to face the center court in an offensive stance. At the next whistle, pivot in the other direction and dribble with the opposite hand.

Coaching points

- Remind your players to always be dribbling with their outer hand, whether it's the left or right.
- More experienced teams can speed up and slow down at the coach's command. The key, however, is to always pick the ball up or put it down quickly after the whistle.

Walking figure 8s

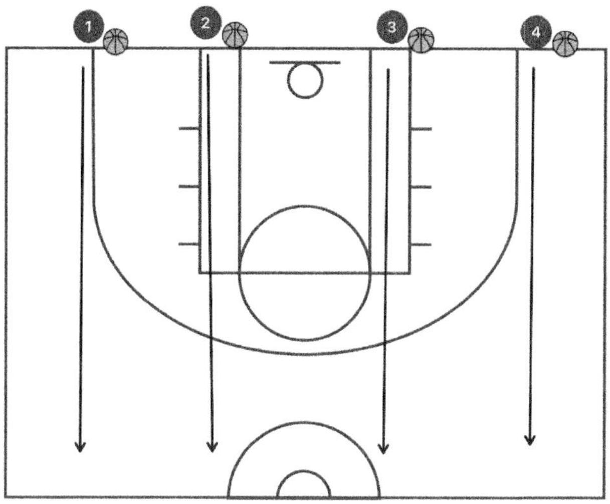

Walking figure 8's

Why it's great

Walking figure 8s serves as a great warm-up for dribbling drills. If your players can execute this drill at speed and without errors, they'll be sure to perform between the legs crossovers with ease.

Setup

Players line up along the baseline, each with a ball.

Instructions

Players stand low and lunge forward. Pass the ball in front of and under the front leg. Step forward and repeat. Do the drill until the half-court line and come back.

Coaching points

- The introduction to this drill would be the stationary figure 8. To make the drill more difficult, dribble the ball low, at ankle height, instead of passing it with the hands.
- Players need to treat this like a dribbling drill and keep their heads up – this drill will teach them to get a feel for coordinating their upper and lower bodies.

Games Based Drills

Dribble knockout

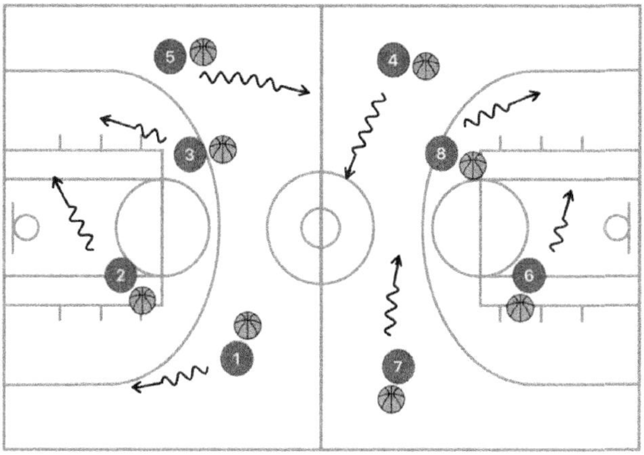

Dribble knockout

Purpose

Improve defensive quickness while mirroring and then into a game of one-on-one for some full-court defense or offense.

Setup

In pairs, players face each other along the key. The coach holds the ball along the baseline.

1. One person is assigned as defensive player and the other is offense.
2. Offense can move left or right and the defensive player must try to stay parallel to the offensive player.
3. The coach throws the ball anywhere, and both players must try to get it.
4. Play one-on-one full court.

Coaching points

The defensive player should stay low in a defensive stance. Try to prevent moving up and down as they are moving laterally.

Variations

Allow the offensive player to move in any direction, but the defender must try to maintain one arm's length distance.

Steal the ball with basketball decision training (BDT)

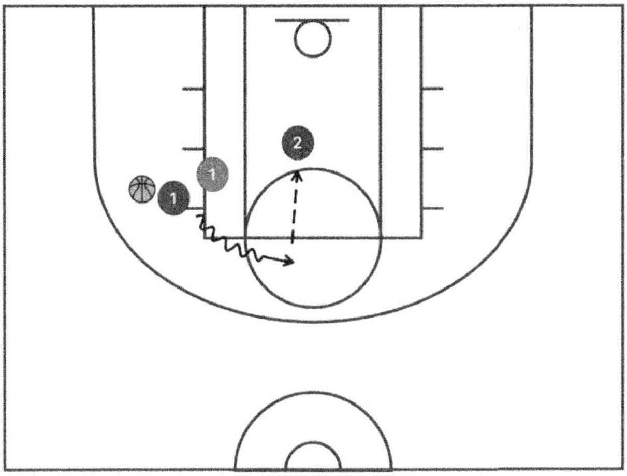

Steal the ball

Why it's great

Steal the ball is already a great drill as it teaches a player how to dribble under pressure. Steal the ball with basketball decision training adds an extra player and makes the drill even more game-like by adding pass decisions.

Setup

Designate a small area, such as the center circle, for your players to play in. Players pair up, one with a ball. A third player or the coach stands on the perimeter.

Instructions

The player with the ball must dribble and protect it against the defender. When the player on the perimeter puts their hands up, the player with the ball must pass to them. Run for five minutes or longer if you prefer and then swap roles.

Coaching points

- To make the drill more difficult, have your players make a dribble move, such as a crossover, every three dribbles.
- Allow your defenders to get as physical as a foul, as this will improve your players' ball security in games and teach them that they won't always get the call.

Two versus two army

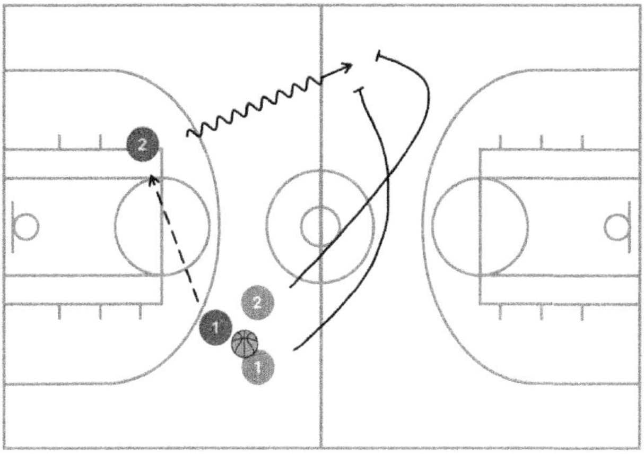

Two versus two army

Purpose

Improve defensive quickness while mirroring, and then into a game of one-on-one for some full-court defense or offense.

Setup

In pairs, players face each other along the key. The coach holds the ball along the baseline.

Instructions

1. One person is assigned as defensive player and the other is offense.
2. Offense can move left or right and the defensive player must try to stay parallel to them.
3. The coach throws the ball anywhere, and both player must try to get it.
4. Play one-on-one full court.

Dribble tag

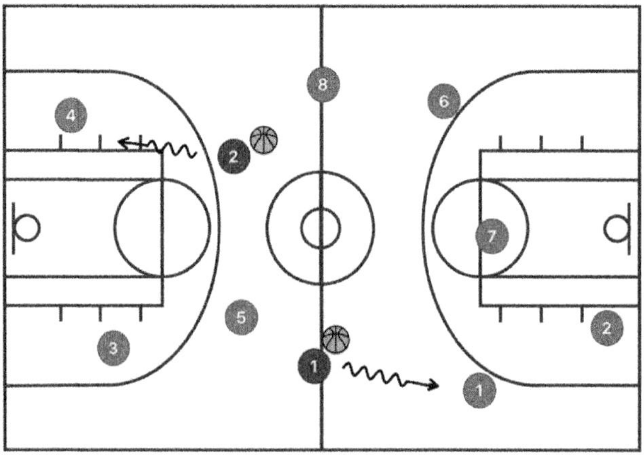

Dribble tag

Why it's great

Who doesn't love a fun dribbling warm-up that'll get your players engaged and active? Dribble tag is a great way to teach ball protection and awareness.

Setup

Each player has a ball and stands inside the three-point line.

Instructions

One player is designated 'it.' On your whistle, players who are 'it' run around and try to tag other players. End when everyone is tagged.

Coaching points

- To make the game more realistic for older players, have the 'it' players steal the opposing player's ball before they are out.
- Practice dribbling with the off-hand by forcing your players to only dribble with that hand.

Contact dribbling

Contact dribbling

Why it's great

Fouls often aren't called and your players need to learn how to play through contact. This drill teaches just that.

Setup

Players start with one ball, facing the coach.

Instructions

Players pound the ball in front of them with one hand. The coach faces them and taps them on their arm, simulating a reach-in foul. Repeat with both hands.

Coaching points

- Advanced players should dribble with two balls, one in each hand.
- Unlike other drills, players shouldn't protect the ball with their body – the aim is to simulate the reach-in foul and to continue dribbling through that initial contact.

Team Drills

Full court off-hand

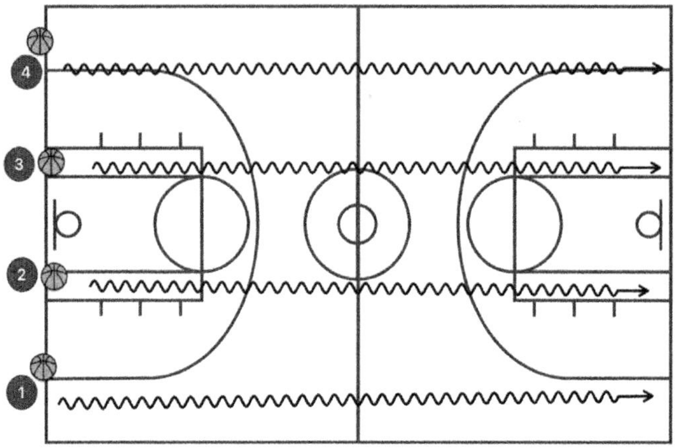

Full court off-hand

Why it's great

Off-hand work is a great way to start practice – at least that's what Coach Collins, three times WI state championship winning coach, thinks. If it's developed the players he's sent to college and the NBA, it should work for your players too.

Setup

Players line up along the baseline, each with a ball.

Instructions

Players dribble from baseline to baseline, using only their off-hand in a series of progressions:

1. V dribbles.
2. In and out.
3. Hesitations.
4. Between the legs.
5. Behind the back.

Work on this progression everyday in practice.

Coaching points

- Young teams should only do four and five to half-court, as crossing over with one hand is quite difficult.
- Once the progression is mastered, players need to begin doing this drill at full speed. Until then, however, stress to them to take their time and keep their heads up.

One vs two press break drill

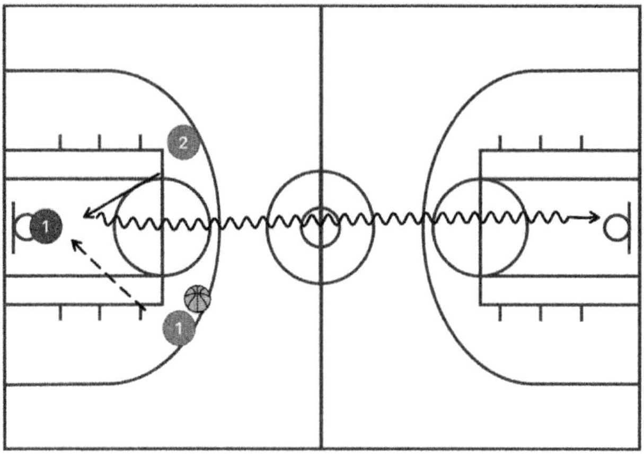

One vs two press break drill

Why it's great

Players get pressed all the time at youth level and the only way to teach them how to handle the pressure is to practice. This drill will teach them to look up, use their body to protect the ball, and use changes of speed to beat the defense.

Setup

Players stand in groups of three along the baseline, one with a ball.

Instructions

Players zigzag their way to half-court. The defense must try to trap the dribble along the baseline. The dribbler must try to avoid getting trapped with changes in speed and direction.

Coaching points

- Initially, players should just do this drill at half-speed, and the defenders allow the dribbler to get to where they want to on the court. This will help them get used to being guarded closely.
- Players on defense need to focus on trapping at 90-degree angles with their hips, not fouling by keeping the hands in the air, and guiding the dribbler to the baseline.

Baseline shuffle and crossover

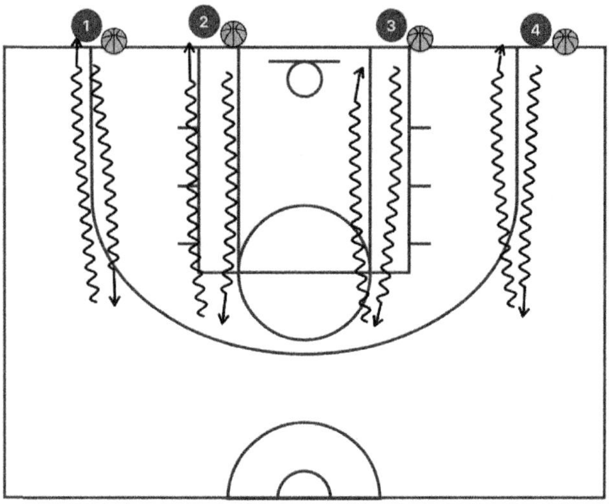

Baseline shuffle and crossover

Why it's great

Protecting the ball is a lost art of dribbling. Drills like these teach players the technique of dribbling the ball under pressure.

Setup

Players line up along the baseline with basketballs.

Instructions

Players face the end of the courtside using their bodies to shield the ball. At the coach's signal, dribble and shuffle forward. At the next signal, they will dribble and shuffle backward. Repeat to the end of the court.

Coaching points

- The movement forward should be quick, the movement back slower. Keep the ball under control at all times.
- Advanced teams should use assistant coaches or another player to harass the dribbler.

Team dribble weapon drill

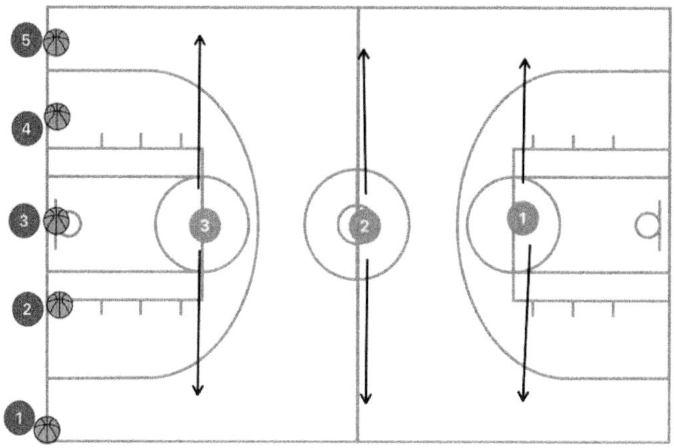

Team dribble

Why it's great

This dribbling drill combines practicing dribble moves with developing them against defenders – a must for any high school team.

Setup

Players line up along the baseline with balls. Three assistant coaches (or players) stand at the top of each perimeter as well as the center circle.

Instructions

The first player dribbles to the first coach, performs a dribble move, and beats him. Repeat with the next coach. At the last coach, they play a one-on-one ending in a layup. When the shot goes up, the next player steps forward.

Coaching points

- The first and second coaches should just guard the player for a few steps then get back in position for the next incoming player.
- Remind your players that the hesitation, not change of direction, is the most effective move in these open court scenarios. Make sure they use it often.

Solo Drills

Tennis ball series

Why it's great

Tennis balls are a fun, cheap tool to improve off-hand coordination. A lot of players forget about their off-hand while dribbling which can be used to protect the ball.

Setup

Every player should have a basketball and a tennis ball.

Instructions

Throw the tennis ball up and catch it while pounding the ball in the other hand.

Progressions

- Throw the ball up and crossover and catch the ball with the other hand.
- Throw the ball up, crossover the ball twice back to original hand, and catch the ball.
- Throw the ball up and do a 360-degree spin.

Side dribbles bounce

Why it's great

This drill is the first of Coach Oliver's side dribbles series. The idea behind it is that players practice a low defensive stance and are also forced to look forward.

Setup

Players stand in front of a coach, each with a ball.

Instructions

Players slide sideways. With each slide, they dribble once, hard, and up to chest height. At the end, crossover and repeat with the other hand.

Coaching points

- Players should keep their heads up, focused on the opposite rim.
- When players are familiar, add in an element of game-based training by having the coach call out changes in direction.

Side dribbles push-pulls

Why it's great

Adding lateral movement to an otherwise stationary drill practices the defensive stance and greater ball control.

Setup

Players stand in front of a coach, each holding a ball.

Instructions

Players slide sideways. With one dribble, they push the ball inwards, and with the next, outwards. At the end, crossover and repeat with the other hand.

Coaching points

- Aim to cover as much distance as possible with each slide. Also aim to dribble the ball inside then outside the body with alternating dribbles.
- Dribble to a steady rhythm

Wall dribbles

Wall dribbles

Why it's great

Using a wall and your player's own hands as a distraction helps keep their eyes off the ball and gets them to develop a feel for dribbling. This is a great drill for younger players.

Setup

Players stand in front of a wall, each with a ball.

Instructions

Players dribble the ball, all the while keeping a hand on the wall. Go through these variations:

1. Dribbling ball at ankle height, hand in place.
2. Dribbling ball while crossing over every two dribbles, swapping hands.
3. Dribbling ball while crossing over behind the back every two dribbles, swapping hands.

Coaching points

- Keep the ball low while dribbling and around the hip, as if they were protecting it in a game.
- Keep the shoulders back and head up at the hand.

Inside out crossover jump shot

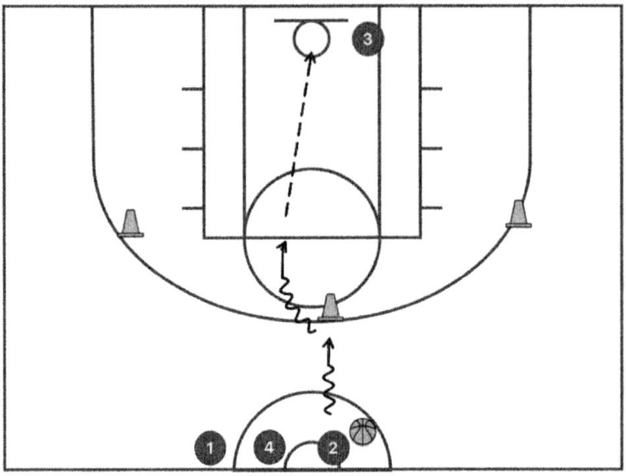

Inside out crossover jump shot

Why it's great

NBA skills coach Don Kelbick is big on spending much of his practice sessions working on one or two key moves. His drills combine shooting and dribbling and are repeated over and over again to become automatic.

Setup

Players stand at half-court with a basketball. Place a cone at the top of the perimeter.

Instructions

Players dribble full speed to the cone and perform an inside out. They then crossover to the other hand, take one dribble, and pull-up and shoot.

Coaching points

- The key to mastering this is repetition from the same spot. Set your players a number of makes per 10 minutes and challenge them to beat their scores.
- Players that aren't typically point guards should do the same drill from the wing – take game shots!

Triple tap crossovers

Triple tap crossovers

Why it's great

Tap the ball three times per crossover. Coach Ryan Holliday of Next Level Basketball loves progressions – packaged sets of drills to develop ball handling that can be run in a 20 minute session per day. This drill is part of his 'killer crossover' series that will see players improve their ball handling, particularly in the pick and roll.

Setup

Players stand in front of a coach, each holding a ball.

Instructions

Players bounce the ball low, at ankle height, three times, and then crossover. Repeat while stationary for one minute.

Coaching points

- This drill will help your players get the ball through traffic but only if they keep the ball low for the triple tap.
- Players shouldn't just bend their back to get low – bend the knees first.

Baby Steps Crossovers

Why it's great

This is another drill in the 'next level' killer crossover series that will increase the speed of your crossovers.

Setup

Players stand in a line, each with a ball.

Instructions

Players walk forward, dribbling the ball at knee height, crossing it over from hand to hand with each dribble.

Coaching points

- Keep the dribble low and the crossovers fast – one with each step forward.
- Try to find a steady rhythm to help you dribble the ball quicker and under control.

Two ball series

Two ball dribbling

Why it's great

Using two balls is another great way to improve both hands at once. Coach Holliday has again designed a great progression and this drill is just a fraction of it.

Setup

Players stand in lines, each holding two balls.

Instructions

Players zigzag. When they change direction, dribble one ball behind the back and one in front, to swap hands. Repeat until half-court.

Coaching points

- Advanced players can alternate between dribbling both balls at once to dribbling balls alternately.
- The secret with this drill is to crossover strong. Bring the hand pushing the ball across the body, otherwise you'll never be able to control the ball.

Figure 8 no dribble into pick up shot

Figure 8 no dribble into pick up shot

Why it's great

Teaching dribble moves is great, but unless they ultimately translate into a shot of some form they're useless. This move helps your players with their ball pick-up skills off the dribble.

Setup

Players stand in the midrange area (or three-point line) with a ball.

Instructions

A player stands in an athletic stance and completes two or four figure 8s between the legs. Hop into a jump shot. Aim to make 20 shots.

Coaching points

- If players are missing the jump shot, make sure they align the ball into their shot pocket (area at chest height where they can bring the ball up directly into a shot).
- Another common mistake is not looking at the basket – the eyes need to preferably be aligned at the hoop throughout the drill, or at least before the ball is brought up to shoot.

10

Shooting and layup drills

"I hate casual shooting. Every shot is preceded by working to get open and catch and shoot under game-like conditions."
– Bob Knight

A basketball player that knows how to score inside, from the midrange, and from the three-point line is a player that will thrive in any system. We know that finding great shooting drills can be hard, which is why we looked through the data from our app, the Practice Planner, to find the 23 best shooting drills that were absolutely loved by you, the coaches.

We have shooting drills in these categories:

- Shooting technique – learn to improve form.
- Game-based shooting – use fun, competitive games to teach shooting.
- Game-ready moves – practice moves your players can use in a game.
- Team shooting – shooting drills to add to your next team

practice.

Shooting technique

Perfect shots

Perfect shots form shooting

Why it's great

Shooting is an art – and perfection is needed from the very first moment you step on the court. Perfect shots makes a great warm-up drill for your players to ensure they enter more complex drills with correct form and the right mindset.

Setup

Players stand along the baseline at the edge of the key, holding a ball in their shooting hand.

Instructions

Players aim and shoot the ball with their shooting hand only. Make three perfect shots in a row – the ball shouldn't touch the rim – then take two steps back. Repeat.

Coaching points

Coach Drew of Coach Market (NCAA div 1 assistant) has a checklist he runs through as he observes his players:

1. Are their feet set and balanced?
2. Is the right foot (for right-hand shooter) slightly in front?
3. Is the elbow bent at 90 degrees and under the ball?
4. Is the shooting arm lined up with the right hip?
5. Is the right foot in line with the middle of the hoop?
6. Is the player looking at the rim?
7. Does the player follow through?

Take note of these seven points each time they shoot.

One-hand set shots close to the rim

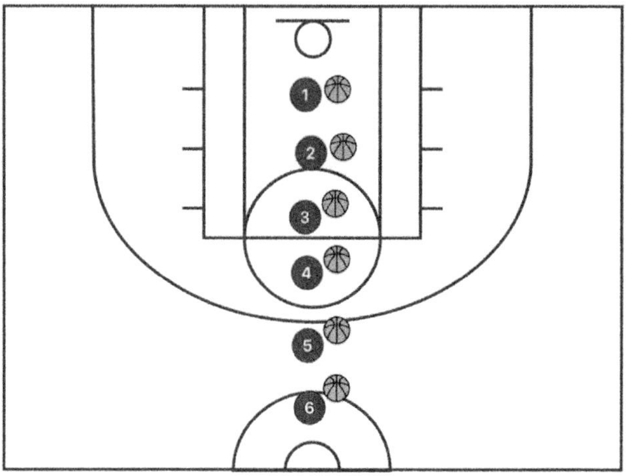

Why it's great

Bob Bigelow, former NBA player and current youth coach, is a big believer in teaching the old school set shot. This drill is for players who are five–eight years old and just beginning to learn shooting form. The set shot makes the movement more simple for players and easier for coaches to focus on technique.

Setup

Players line up in front of the rim, no more than 10 ft (3 m) away. Bigelow also recommends that for young kids coaches should try to use a rim that is 8–9 ft (2.4–2.7 m) high, and use a smaller size four (25.5 in/65 cm) basketball. This prevents players from making the number one mistake of chucking or heaving the ball.

Instructions

Players take a set shot, aiming for the back of the rim. Run for five minutes or longer if you prefer.

Coaching points

- Coaches shouldn't focus on the makes or misses, but rather on the form – no chucking, make sure they are bending their knees, shooting with an extended follow through.
- Players should rotate their hips slightly so that their shooting foot is in front rather than being directly square on.

180 pivot form shooting

180 pivot form shooting

Why it's great

In games, players often have to quickly face the basket, find their balance, and fire off a shot – particularly off cuts from the middle or in the post. This drill practices this fundamental skill.

Setup

Players stand 10 ft (3 m) from the hoop, facing away from the basket.

Instructions

Players pivot off the front foot, aiming to square up and fire off a jump shot as quickly as possible. Try to make 10 in a row and move around with each shot.

Coaching points

- Make the drill more difficult by only counting perfect swishes. In addition, practice pivoting off both feet.
- This is a form shooting drill so don't worry about elevating – focus on balance and a quick shot release.

One-foot hop into a shot

Why it's great

One-foot hops into a shot is a great way to stimulate receiving a pass without a passer. It forces players to learn how to 'fight for their feet' and get into the rhythm of their shot.

Setup

Players stand at the free-throw line with a ball.

Instructions

Players stand on one foot and hop three times. On the third hop they try to bring their raised foot down as quickly as possible and shoot. Make 20 and swap feet.

Coaching points

- Once mastered, players can add variations, such as a one-dribble pull-up, to their shot.
- An extra benefit of the hop is making sure players are activating their legs in the shot. Be sure that they are stable and jumping in one spot.

Random Mikan

Random Mikan

Why it's great

This re-envisioning of the classic Mikan drill (named after the pro NBL player George Mikan), adds an element of randomness into a proven layup drill. In games, players rarely attack the basket from the same angle each time, so this drill teaches them to be creative and have balance when finishing.

Setup

Players stand under the hoop with a ball.

Instructions

Players shoot a layup and rebound the ball. Repeat the drill on the other side of the basket. The two rules are: 1. Players must alternate shooting between left and right hands 2. No two consecutive shots can be the same. Players must make 10 layups in a row or try to make 30 in a minute.

Coaching points

- Examples of different types of layups include two-footed power layups, traditional layups, off-footed layups, floaters, and reverse layups.
- The key to this drill is that players should always have their eyes on the rim.

Game-based shooting

Beanbag shooting

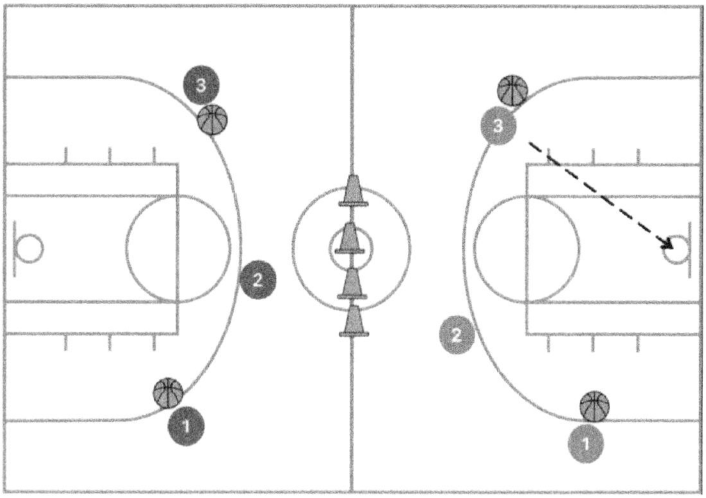

Beanbag shooting

Why it's great

This is the ultimate shooting game from Ron Yeung of Canada Basketball that combines shooting, dribbling, shooting under pressure, and at game speed. Each time a player gets a shot in, they can collect a beanbag/cone from the center line. They can also steal a beanbag from the opposing team. The first team to reach a certain number wins!

Setup

Place an odd number of cones in the center of the court. Start with seven and then add more as your players get better. Give one ball to each player and separate into two teams on each half of the court.

Instructions

Make as many three-pointers in a row as possible before missing two in a row.

Coaching points

There are multiple ways to increase the difficulty of this drill:

- Make your players dribble to collect a cone. Use weak hand or alternate hands.
- Time the length of the game.
- If a player misses, dribble the length of the court before they can take another shot.
- Increase distance, from outside key to three-pointers.
- Add active defenders from the opposing team to try to steal the balls.
- In pairs, players cannot dribble to collect a cone and can only advance by passing to each other.

Beat the Pro

Why it's great

This drill puts pressure on the shooter and brings out their competitive side to focus on their form. Tell your players the scores of NBA players (below) and get them to aim for that goal.

Setup

Pick a three-point spot. Find a rebounder and start shooting!

Instructions

Make as many three-pointers in a row as possible before missing two in a row.

Coaching points

Here's a list of current records by pro players your kids can aim for:

- Steph Curry – 76
- Klay Thompson – 122
- Marcus Paige – 156
- Buddy Hield – 197
- Joel Berry II – 251

Two-player basketball decision training

Two-player basketball decision training shooting

Why it's great

Basketball decision training was designed by Coach Oliver of the University of Windsor Men's Lancers as a system to teach his players to read and react instantly to the defense. It teaches players to respond to a series of cues that mimic a game – it is a great drill for many motion offenses.

Setup

Players pair up with an assistant coach or another player. They start by standing on the perimeter with a ball.

Instructions

A player stands with the ball and is prepared to respond to one of the following cues in the other player:

1. Arms out – pass the ball.
2. Step toward – drive and layup.
3. Arms down – shoot.
4. Jump to the side – drive, crossover, and floater in middle.
5. Hands out step toward – give and go.
6. Hands out on drive – drive and kick.

Run for a total of 20 made baskets and then swap positions.

Coaching points

- Ease the players into the progressions – teach one at a time with lots of repetitions.
- Stress that it's important to develop a quick reaction to the signal.

Three players two balls

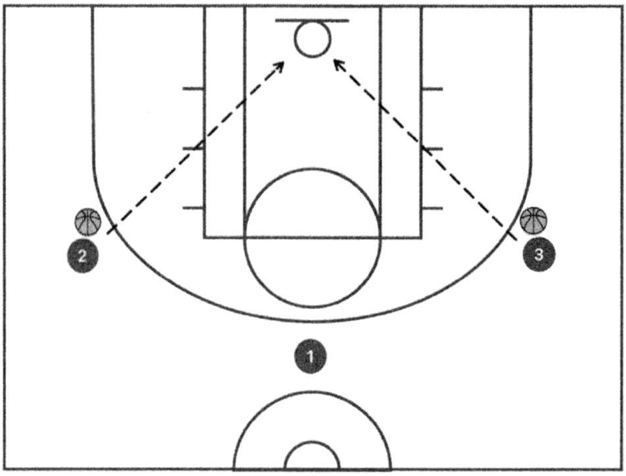

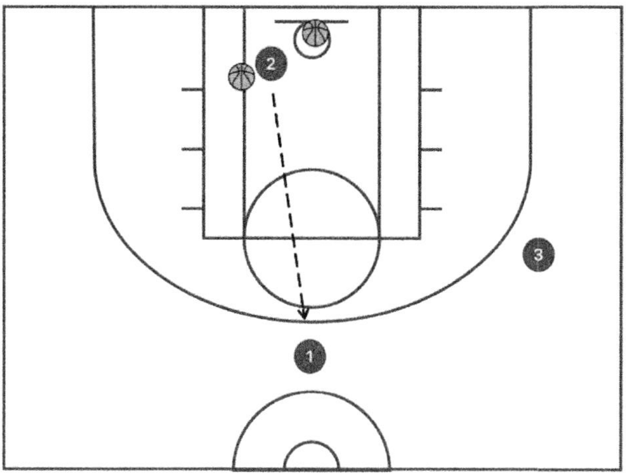

Shooters get own rebound and then pass to an open man

Why it's great

A drill that works on shooting from different positions, conditioning and passing at game speed. Shooters shoot, get rebound, and pass to the open player. After the pass, run to open spot for the shot.

Setup

Two balls and three players per hoop.

Instructions

1. Three players start in positions they want to shoot from.

2. Shoot the basketball.
3. Grab the rebound (hit or miss).
4. Pass to open man.
5. Relocate to next shot location.
6. Receive a pass and shoot again.

Coaching points

- Shoot at game speed. Catch the ball and then immediately shoot.
- Stress perfect passes to the shooting pocket of the shooter.

Two-man chaser layups

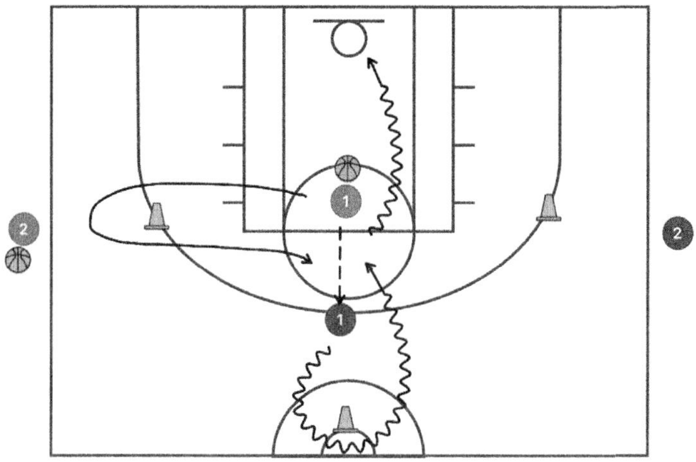

Two-man chaser layup

Why it's great

Players will have to deal with pressure from defenders when attempting transition layups. This drill has them coming from multiple angles and teaches awareness and composure.

Setup

Players pair up, and these pairs line up one either side of the key. Two cones are set up at the wings. One player has a ball.

Instructions

Players sprint to circle around their nearest cones. The three defenders try to pressure the one player with the ball. Swap lines after a shot and repeat for 25 team makes.

Coaching points

- The on-ball defender should start on the outside of the dribbler.
- Players defending on-ball should aim to provide pressure only (it is difficult to block from behind without fouling). The weak side defenders can attempt to block the ball.

Slalom layups

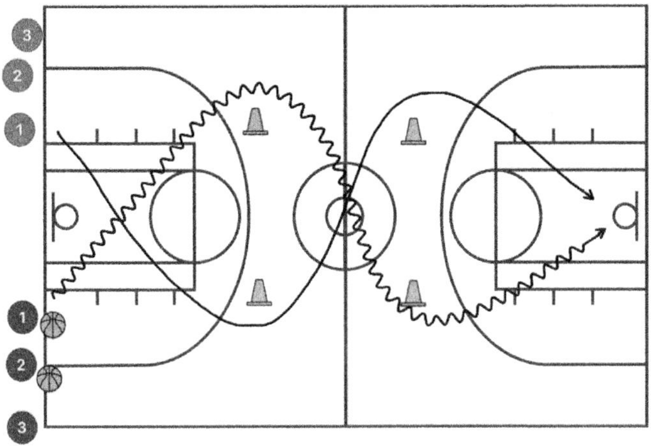

Slalom layups

Why it's great

If you've been watching the top two drills closely, you'll realize that they all have something in common. These three drills were designed by game-based guru Brian McCormick and are fun, competitive ways to teach critical finishing skills.

Setup

Place two cones 15 ft (4.5 m) apart at the free-throw lines and half-court lines. Players start at one end, and one has a ball.

Instructions

The players weave in and out of the cones. The player with the ball tries to make a layup at the other end. Run for 25 makes.

Coaching points

- To make the drill more difficult, increase the number of cones players need to move around.
- You can also add an extra help defender under the basket to add to the challenge.

Game ready moves

One-dribble pull-up

One-dribble pull-up

Why it's great

Most players can only shoot off the catch. Make sure you can also shoot off the dribble.

Setup

Players stand along the perimeter with a ball.

Instructions

Players spin the ball to themselves to stimulate a pass. After catching the ball, players take one dribble and pull-up. Repeat for five makes each side.

Coaching points

- The one dribble needs to be hard as it helps you beat the defender and rise up to shoot.
- The dribble should take the player from the perimeter to just behind the free-throw line.

Step away running jump shot

Step away running jump shot

Why it's great

The Euro step is a great move and you can also use it further away from the basket to create space for a jump shot. Push off the inside foot to create space and then shoot.

Setup

Players stand along the perimeter with a ball.

Instructions

Players spin the ball to themselves to stimulate a pass. After catching the ball, players take one dribble and pull-up. Repeat for five makes each side.

Coaching points

- The one dribble needs to be hard as it helps you beat the defender and rise up to shoot.
- The dribble should take the player from the perimeter to just behind the free-throw line.

Turn out double change layup

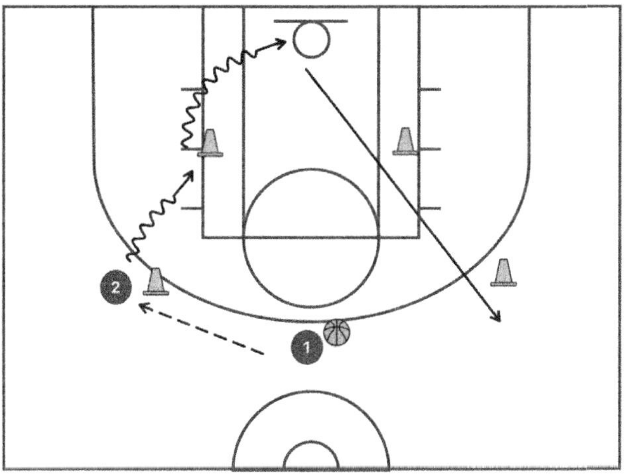

Turn out double change layup

Why it's great

Don Kelbick designed this move as part of his wing perimeter player series. It is a great counter for defenders that aren't beaten by the first step.

Setup

A coach stands at the top with a ball, a player stands under the basket, and a cone is at the wing.

Instructions

The player cuts to the wing and catches the pass, turning out with an inside pivot. They explode off a first step, then hesitate. Crossover twice and drive to the outside and layup.

Coaching points

- This move is reliant on the hesitation to freeze the defender. It is possibly even more important than a quick double crossover.
- Once mastered, practice with a crossover step and an outside pivot.

Curry pull up

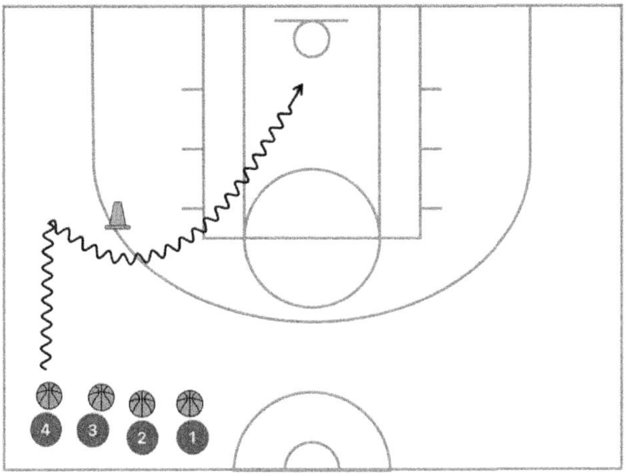

Curry pullup

Why it's great

Former Utah and Team Canada player Tyler Kepkay breaks down the secret to Steph Curry's pull-up – and it's not just a simple one-two into a shot.

Setup

Players start at the half-court with a ball. Cones are laid out at the wing to mimic a screen.

Instructions

The shooter dribbles to the wing position, then takes a hard inside-out dribble with the inner hand. They then either take the shot or go around the cones to a two-dribble pull-up in the lane.

Coaching points

- Foot work is important in this – during the inside-out dribble the player must fake going outside the screen, then use their feet to move completely across the screen, driving the defender into it.
- Run this pull-up at full speed – even the run from half-court is important because the hesitation before the in and out can freeze a defender.

LeBron step backs

LeBron step backs

Why it's great

A step-back after dribbling between the legs is one of LeBron's signature moves. It may look awkward but the diagonal step-back can throw defenders off and create space.

Setup

Players stand in the wing in the midrange area with a basket-ball.

Instructions

Players dribble stationary, then crossover between the legs from inside to out. Gather and shoot. Make 10 going from right to left and 10 from left to right.

Coaching points

- Emphasize that the movement is not just a step backward but also sideways in the direction of the crossover.
- Keep your eyes on the hoop at all times.

Team-based shooting

OSU shooting drill

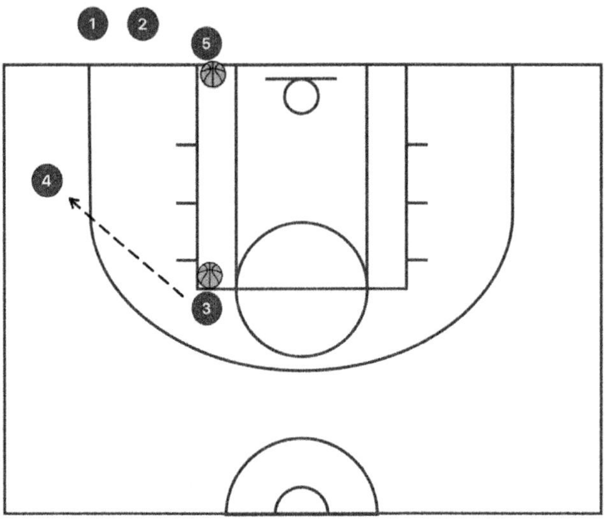

Pass the ball to the wing

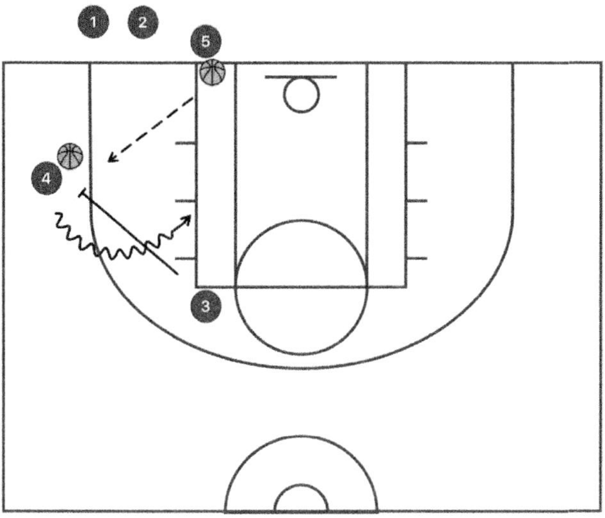

Set a ball screen and then receive a pass for the shot

Why it's great

This is a variation of the drill above designed by Coach Ryan Holliday of Next Level Basketball. It is an efficient team-shooting drill designed to incorporate game skills such as shooting off screens.

Setup

Players line up under the basket with basketballs. A player starts at the wing with a basketball, and another player stands at the top.

Instructions

The player at the top sets a screen for the player with the ball. They use it, driving middle, and dribble to the elbow to shoot. The screener flares to the corner and catches and shoots. Run for 25 team makes.

Coaching points

- Make sure players run this drill at game pace.
- They also need to use the screen properly and brush shoulders. Do not just go through the motions.

Chair work - elbows

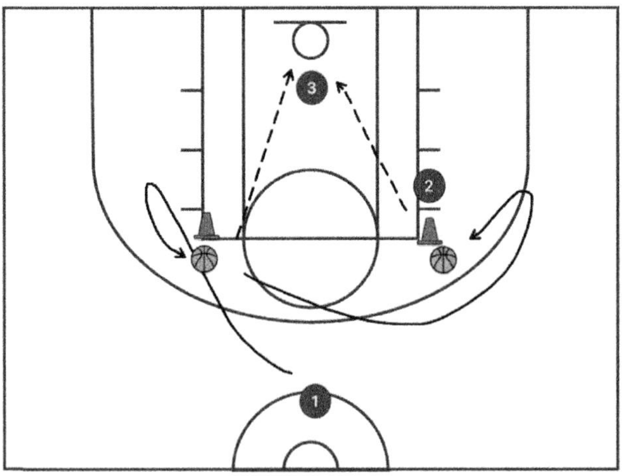

Chair shooting

Why it's great

This is another awesome drill by Next Level that gets in repetitions at a common shooting spot – the elbows. The use of chairs allows for balls to be always there and activates the legs as players have to bend lower to collect the ball.

Setup

Place two chairs with balls on them at the elbows, and two rebounders stand behind them. The shooter stands at the free-throw line.

Instructions

The shooter runs past the elbow, fakes a backdoor cut, then curls around to get the ball from the elbow chair. Pick up and shoot. Run for 20 makes then swap shooters.

Coaching points

- The footwork off the fake cut is vital – after faking, pivot off the upper inside foot to immediately run back. Don't waste time bringing the outer foot around.
- If players are having difficulty picking the ball up from the chair, try rolling it out first before holding it.

Slot shooting drill

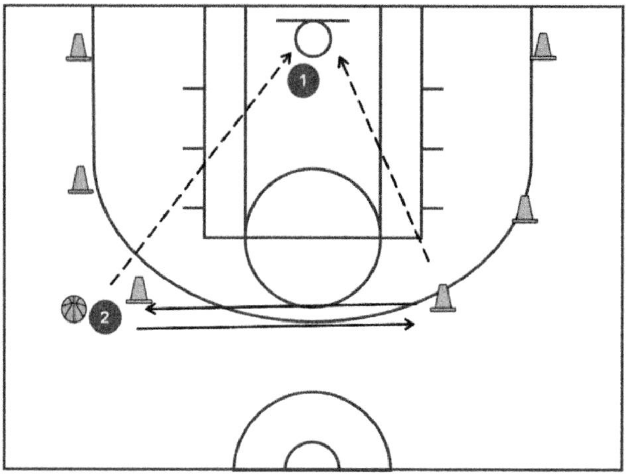

Slot shooting drill

Why it's great

The 'slot' is a position on the perimeter between the top and the wing is an area of scoring popularized by Steph Curry. This drill works on shooting from there and also doubles as a conditioning drill.

Setup

A player stands in the slot, and a rebounder stands under the basket with a ball.

Instructions

The shooter catches and shoots, then runs to the opposite slot. After four makes, repeat the drill at the wings, and then the corners.

Coaching points

- Players must not cheat by running straight to their point – they must circle the perimeter to shoot.
- Add a time element – give players a two-minute limit to make 12 shots.

Mirror drill into one-on-one

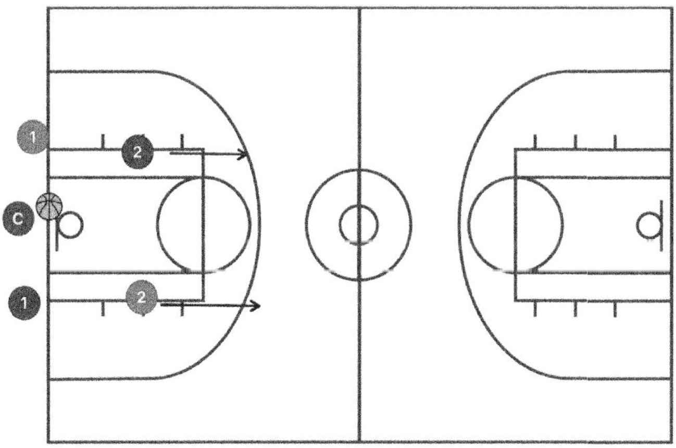

Play defensive mirror

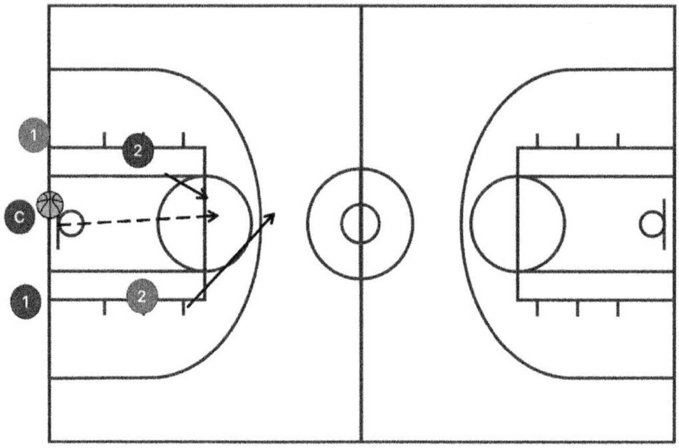

Coach throws ball out

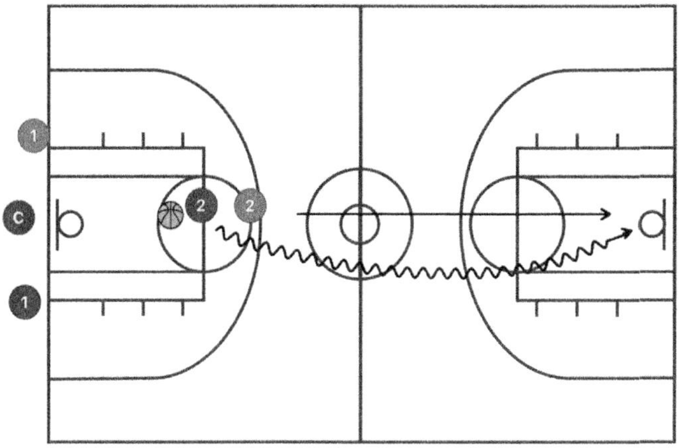

One-on-one full court

Why it's great

Improve defensive quickness while mirroring and then into a game of one-on-one for some full-court defense or offense.

Setup

In pairs, players face each other along the key. The coach holds the ball along the baseline.

Instructions

1. One person is assigned as defensive player and one as offense.

2. Offense can move left or right and the defensive player must try to stay parallel to them.
3. The coach throws the ball anywhere, and both players must try to get it.
4. Play one-on-one full court.

Coaching points

The defensive player should stay low in a defensive stance. Try to prevent moving up and down as they are moving laterally.

Variations

Allow the offensive player to move in any direction – the defender must try to maintain one arm's length distance.

11

Passing drills

Passing is possibly the most neglected fundamental skill of basketball. Often a coach will show players passing drills when they're learning the game, then never go back to them for the rest of their basketball career.

Think of the reasons why the San Antonio Spurs, Golden State Warriors, and Team USA run passing drills every day in practice. Think of all the components to a pass that turn a turnover into an assist: vision, accuracy, precision, timing, and speed. A pass needs to be on target to the same degree of precision as a jump shot, and we make many more passes in a game than jump shots. Despite this, I'm willing to bet that there's a very good chance 90 percent of the coaches out there will work on shooting for one hour and passing for about 10 minutes.

If you're coaching a new or very young team, we recommend the 'learn to pass' drills to teach technique. We've also got age-appropriate drills for coaches of a specific level of school team that you can easily incorporate into practice. Finally, as always we're a big believer in game-based practice – we think that the randomness of game-based passing drills develop creativity and awareness in a way that 'traditional' drills can't. These include:

- Learn to pass for U9s and beginners.
- Game-based passing for all ages.
- Elementary and middle school team passing for U11s and U14s.
- AAU and high school team passing for U16s and U18s.

Learn to pass

Wall chest pass

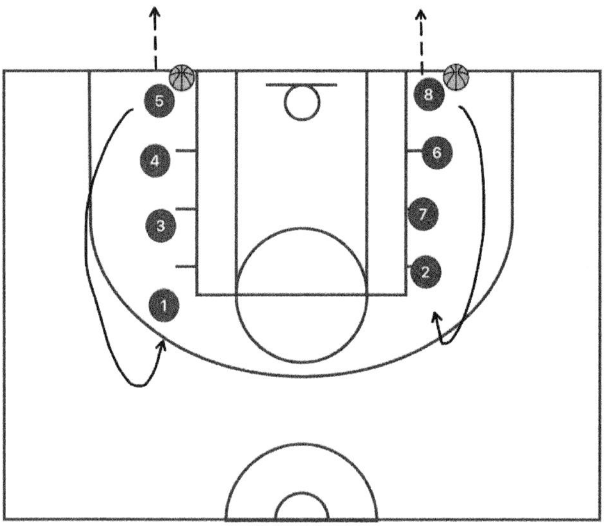

Why it's great

This drill teaches young players how to pass accurately. If your players don't hit the same spot each time, you'll be immediately aware of it as they'll be running left and right.

Setup

Give each player a ball and have them stand about 5 ft (1.5 m) away from a wall.

Instructions

Players stand still and throw a pass off the wall at a height where it will come back to their chest. Throw 20 passes.

Coaching points

- Players need to make a 'W' with their hands to hold the ball – fingers wrapped around the ball, thumbs pointing inwards, slightly apart.
- Very young players may need to throw the ball above their head as they may not be strong enough to throw a pass that will rebound with enough force.

Variations

- Players can stand back and add a step inwards with the pass once they've mastered the hand coordination.
- A team variation of the drill is to have players stand in a

line. The first player passes and runs to the back of the line while the second collects the rebound and passes again.

Close wall passing

Close wall passing

Why it's great

Strength is as much a problem as coordination for young players. This drill works both and also teaches the basketball fundamental that we do everything with our fingertips.

Setup

Players stand 1 ft (30 cm) away from a wall with a basketball.

Instructions

Players hold the ball above their head and bounce it quickly off the wall with one hand. Make 25 in a row on each side.

Coaching points

- Players need to stand side-on for this drill. Make sure that the wrist, elbow, and shoulder are all aligned at right angles.
- If players find it difficult to concentrate on one spot, make a marking on the wall that they have to hit.

Variations

- Once players have mastered the accuracy element have them move the ball in small circles around the wall.

Chest pass with ball fakes and pivots

Why it's great

Pivoting, not dribbling, is the first thing a player should do after catching a pass. What this drill does is teach young players this good habit while using the correct footwork.

Setup

Players pair up and line up facing each other, 15 ft (4.5 m) apart. One line holds the balls.

Instructions

Players run 5 ft (1.5 m) and receive a pass from their teammate. They shot fake, then pivot 180 degrees, pause, then pivot to face their teammate again. Return the pass and shuffle backward. Repeat for 10 passes and swap roles.

Coaching points

- Players need to catch the ball in a position ready to shoot. That means that the right foot (for a right-handed shooter) should be in front. A right-handed shooter should also pivot anti-clockwise around the back foot.
- "Be quick but don't hurry" – this is a quote from player and coach John Wooden used by Bob Bigelow to describe how your players should treat this drill. Their pivots need to be quick but under control.

Passing and lateral shuffle drill

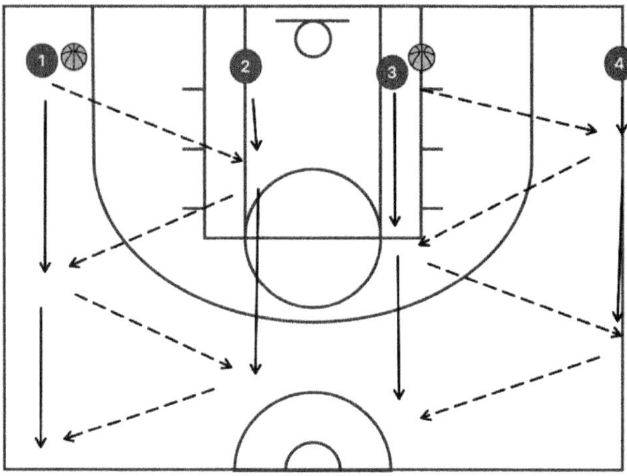

Why it's great

Stationary passing drills are great to teach technique, but basketball isn't played standing still. This drill will teach players the important concept of 'leading' their passes in front of their teammate.

Setup

Players pair up, facing each other 10 ft (3 m) apart. One player has a ball.

Instructions

Players pass the ball to their partner, then shuffle laterally. Repeat to the halfway line and return.

Coaching points

If players are having difficulty shuffling in a line, get them to follow lines on the court. The baseline to volleyball boundary line is one such option.

Variations

- Once the chest pass is mastered, have them throw bounce, one handed, and overhead passes.

Games based passing

Zigzag passing

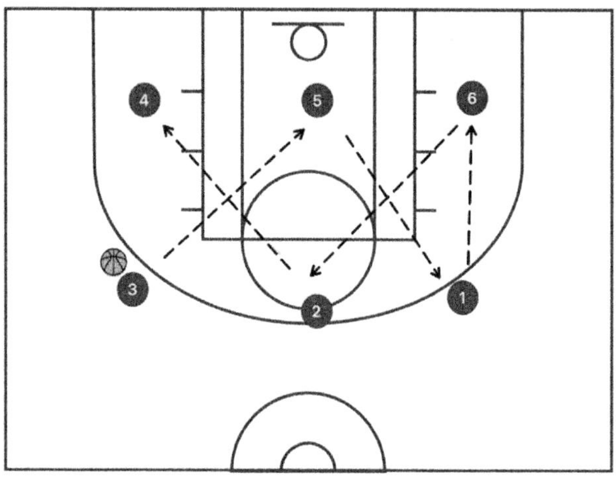

Why it's great

This is a basic passing game, good for kids aged nine and under. The players are stationary, allowing them to work on accuracy and passing form.

Setup

Players stand in two lines, each line is 10 ft (3 m) apart and the players spread out about an arm's length from each other.

Instructions

Players pass the ball to the player diagonally opposite them. Repeat to one end of the line and then head back.

Coaching points

- Young players may feel tempted to throw one handed, underarm, or bounce passes. Make sure that they are passing with the correct technique.
- Tell young players to aim for their partner's chest when passing.

Variations

- Split the team up into two groups and run a relay race. The first to pass the ball back up and down the line wins.
- Older, more experienced players can run the same drill for the length of the court and with two or more balls.

Team passing tag

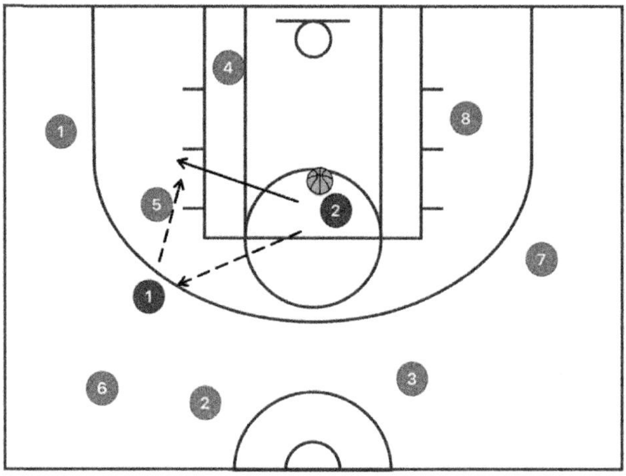

Why it's great

This passing drill specifically emphasizes quick ball movement – your players won't be able to win if they don't work as a team to pass the ball around.

Setup

Players split into two teams, one of catchers and one of runners. The catchers have the balls.

Instructions

The catchers try to tag the runners, but they can only tag them with the basketball. The ball cannot be thrown to tag players and the catchers cannot dribble or run with the ball. Play until everyone is caught, then swap roles.

Coaching points

- Smart teams will figure out that one person needs to be trailing the target runner at all times.
- Reinforce the idea that quick ball movement and good communication is key to success.

Variations

- Young players that aren't so adept at passing can have the game made easier by allowing one dribble or reducing the size of the court.

Monkey in the middle

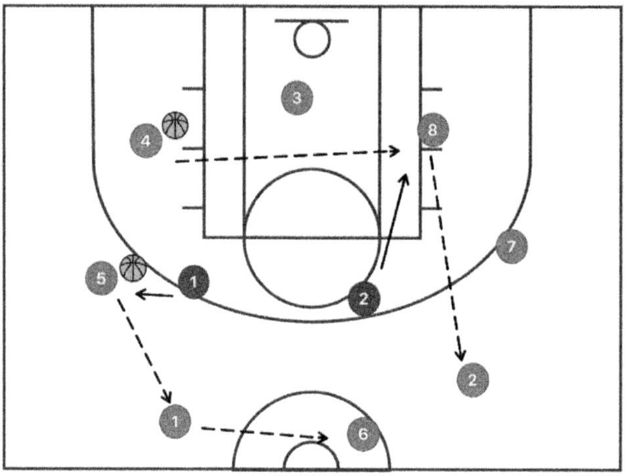

Why it's great

Classic monkey in the middle is an example of a bad drill for young players. Long story short, there's a lot standing around and not enough touches for all the players. This variation on monkey in the middle changes that.

Setup

Players split into groups of three – one is the monkey, the other two are the players. The monkey stands between the players, each roughly 7 ft (2.1 m) apart.

Instructions

The players must try to make 10 consecutive passes between them. If the monkey steals the ball, they swap out with the player.

Coaching points

Young players will be tempted to throw one-handed passes – don't let them! Their hands are too small to do that. There are many two-handed ways to evade the defender, such as overhead, bounce passes, and passing around the monkey.

Variations

- If players are finding the game too easy, eliminate lob passes.
- If you do want to play the game with a large group, try to increase the number of balls as well as the defenders. This means that players will have to use off-ball cutting to get open.

Long Island passing drill

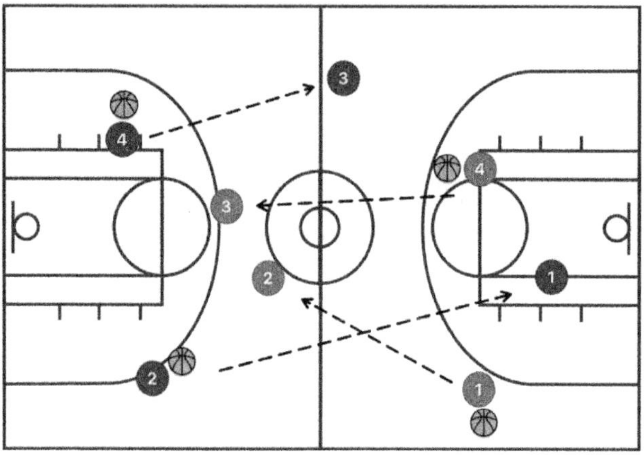

Why it's great

This drill doesn't have the pressure of defense yet still creates an environment where players will be forced to be aware and communicate clearly.

Setup

Players split into groups of five. Each group stands in a large circle and has a ball. The circles should overlap, similar to the Olympic rings pattern.

Instructions

Players pass the ball to someone far away from them in the circle. They then must cut to an open space in another circle. Run this drill for five minutes or longer if you prefer.

Coaching points

- If young players are having difficulty knowing where to cut, mark the circles out with cones on the ground.
- Passing should be quick – players should never hold on to the ball for too long.

Variations

- Make the game more difficult by having players change the size of the circle i.e. move in or move out while it is going on.
- Also, try adding in new balls once players are familiar with the drill.

Four-on-four volleyball passing

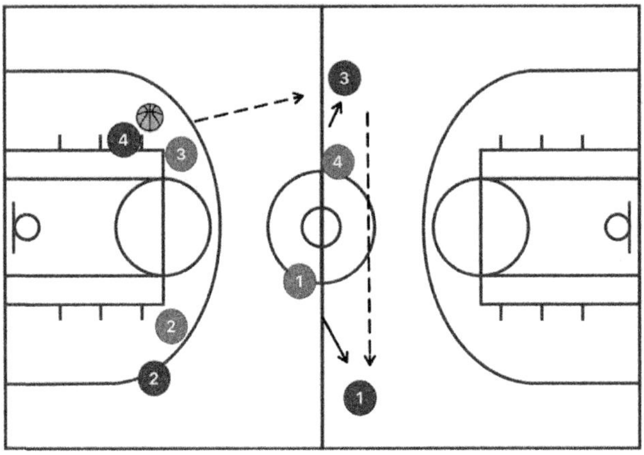

Why it's great

This is a fun passing game that forces players to make decisions.

Setup

Two teams of four players spread out in a defined area.

Instructions

1. The offensive team must try to make 10 passes in a row.
2. The defensive team is trying to intercept the ball.

3. The offensive team can move within the defined area except the person with the ball.

Coaching points

Try to teach different types of passes: bounce, overheard, behind the ball, and chest passes for example.

Variations

Adjust the difficulty by:

- Changing the area to a bigger zone to make it easier, or smaller to make the drill harder.
- If necessary, force defenders to double-team the ball to make it easier.
- Force the passes to pass within two seconds of holding the ball.

Seven versus five passing

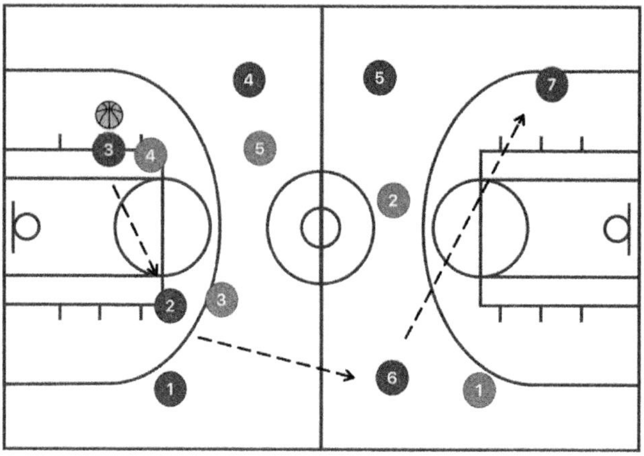

Why it's great

Another great passing game that creates a numbers advantage for the offense.

Setup

In a defined area, have seven players on offense and five players on defense.

Instructions

1. The seven person offensive team has to make 10 passes in a row.
2. The defensive team tries to steal the ball.
3. Everyone apart from the person with the ball can move.

Coaching points

With more players, it gets more important to have spacing. You can create spacing by passing and then moving instead of standing still. Also, spread out and use the space as much as possible.

Variations

- Change the difficulty of the game by increasing or decreasing number of defenders.
- Increase or decrease the size of area the players can move into.
- Limit the time a passer can hold the ball for.
- Disallow passes back to the person who passed to you.
- Disallow overhead passes.

Elementary and middle school team passing drills

Square passing

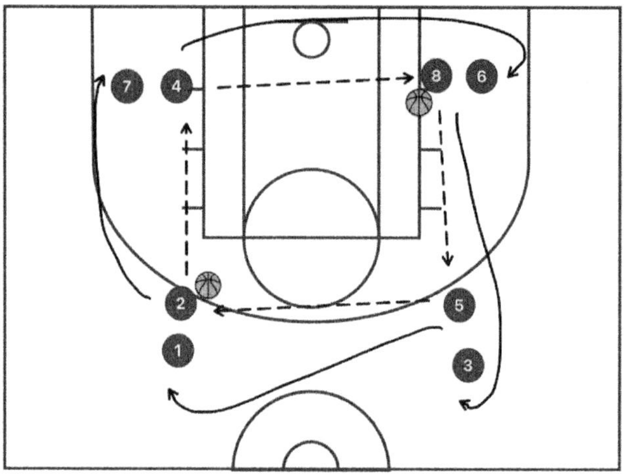

Why it's great

Young players will learn to pass quickly and with accuracy. The hallmarks of a great young team is being able to run this drill without any mistakes.

Setup

Players stand in lines in square, each line about 12 ft (3.6 m) apart. The first player in one line has the ball.

Instructions

The player passes the ball clockwise and follows the pass to cut to the end of the line. Run for five minutes or longer if you prefer.

Coaching points

Emphasize being prepared to catch the basketball – knees bent, body angled toward the passer, and arms up.

Variations

- Add a second ball to the game, which will speed the drill up.
- Advanced players can also use this as a conditioning drill, reducing the number of players in each line to two and counting the number of passes done.

Basic triangles and cuts to the basket

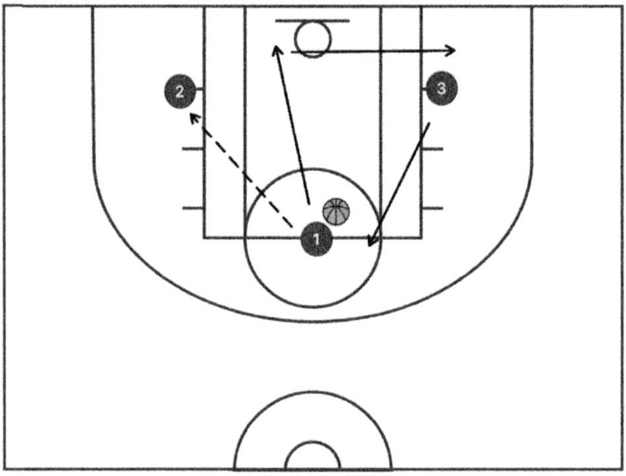

Why it's great

This drill teaches many great team passing principles – cutting to the basket, cutting into space along the perimeter, and how to give and go.

Setup

Players split up into groups of three. One player stands at the top of the key with a basketball, two players stand at the wings.

Instructions

The player at the top passes the ball to a player at the wing, and then cuts to the basket. The opposite wing slides up to the top to fill the space. The wing player with the ball returns it to the top, who passes it back to the cutter who has now popped back out.

Coaching points

- Add the pass to the cutter for a layup only once players have mastered the passing movement.
- Communication is key to this drill – get your players to shout out that they want the ball.

Variations

- You can add three defenders to provide some pressure for the players.
- Play three-on-three where an extra point is given for scoring off a give and go

Two-lane passing

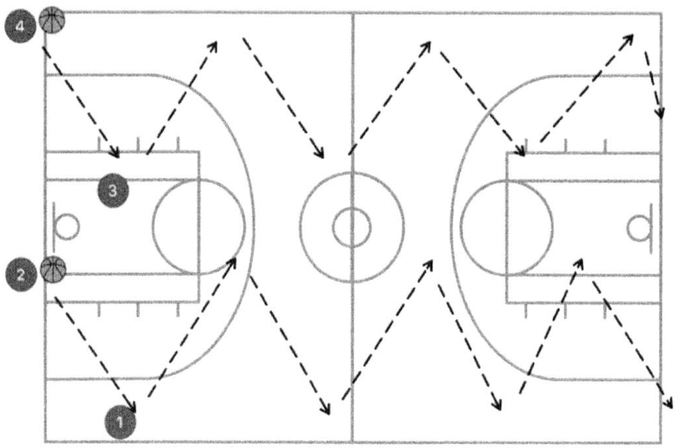

Why it's great

This drill teaches players to run with their hands up and keep their spacing – vital skills for a super quick fast break.

Setup

Players pair up and stand in two lines along the baseline, one at the corner three area and another just outside the key.

Instructions

Players pass the ball and run. Repeat to the end of the court and return.

Coaching points

- Players need to keep their spacing. Make sure that they don't deviate from the line.
- Spread your players out into two lines of two to maximize space.

Variations

- Have your players repeat the drill if the get it wrong – there should be no mistakes.
- Use this drill as conditioning or as part of your warm-up.

Two balls, three players passing

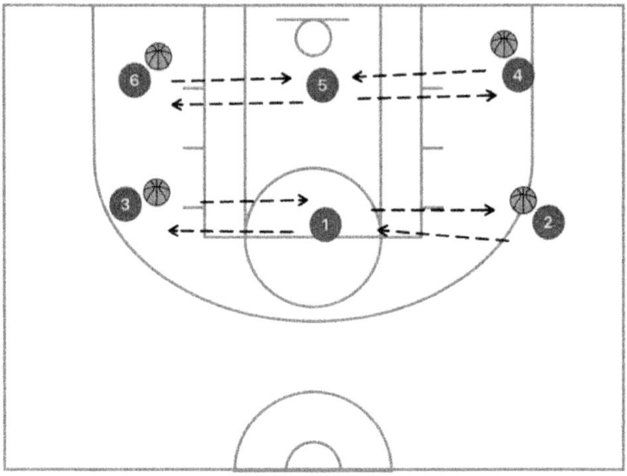

Why it's great

This is a drill that will reinforce correct passing and pivoting technique – great for younger players.

Setup

Players split into groups of three. They stand in a line, 10 ft (3 m) apart. The side players have the balls.

Instructions

The middle player catches and returns a pass. They pivot 180 degrees and do the same. Repeat for 20 passes and then do it again while pivoting on the other leg.

Coaching points

- Remind your players to keep the legs bent as they pivot.
- The pressure is on the passers to be aware and fire the pass in as soon as the other player pivots.

Variations

- You can do the drill with three passers and two balls, all facing in front of the player. The central passer will have to catch the pass and then pivot to pass to the player without the ball.

High school team passing

Italian drill

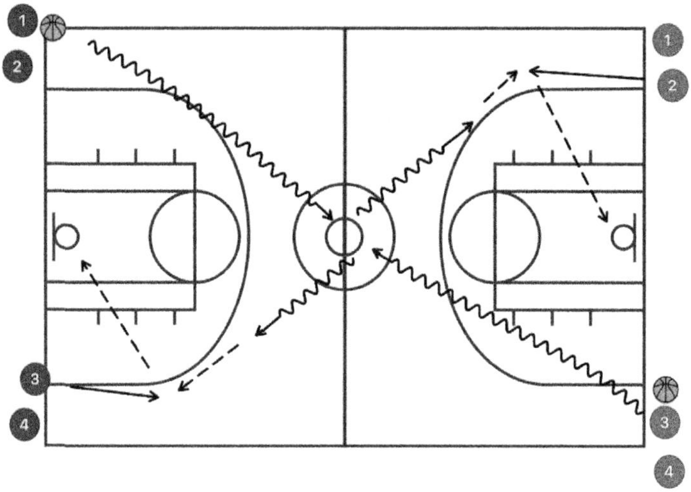

Why it's great

Coach Chris Oliver of the University of Windsor Lancers runs this drill as a warm-up as it is an excellent fit for his zero-seconds dribble-drive offense. If you run a similar offense, consider using this drill as well!

Setup

Players line up at diagonally opposite baselines, each with a ball. One player stands at the wing furthest away from the line.

Instructions

The first player dribbles to half-court, crosses over, and then approaches the top. They throw a pass to the player on the wing, who shoots the three.

Coaching points

Players need to pass off the dribble with one hand (the outer hand), as this is a quicker pass that will be harder to intercept.

Variations

- Have the wing player drive and kick back out to the incoming passer. The passer then shoots the three.

Hall of fame drill

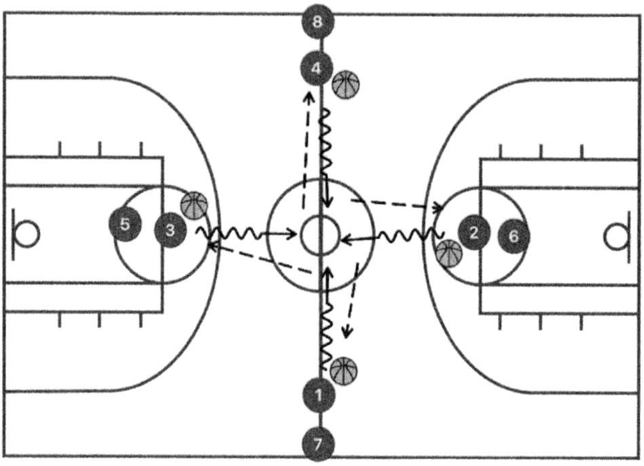

Why it's great

Players that don't pivot properly will make turnovers in open court and half-court situations. You must teach your players to use the pivot effectively to go around the defender.

Setup

Players line up in four lines. Two lines face each other so that they are organized like a '+.' The first player in each line has the ball.

Instructions

Players dribble to the center, jump stop and pivot toward a line, and pass. Do the following pivots (this drill presumes that the player is a right-handed shooter, with right foot in front):

1. Pivot off the front foot.
2. Reverse pivot off the back foot.
3. Reverse pivot off the front foot.
4. Double pivot – pivot 180 degrees one way then swing around and pass.

Coaching points

- Players need to keep their stance low, knees bent, to pivot correctly.
- Players may get confused with the direction of their pivoting. Let them show initiative to talk and figure it out.

Variations

One way to make the drill more game-based once players have mastered the variations is to let players pivot how they want, but they cannot repeat the same pivot that was done before them, and they cannot pass to a player with a ball.

Halo passing

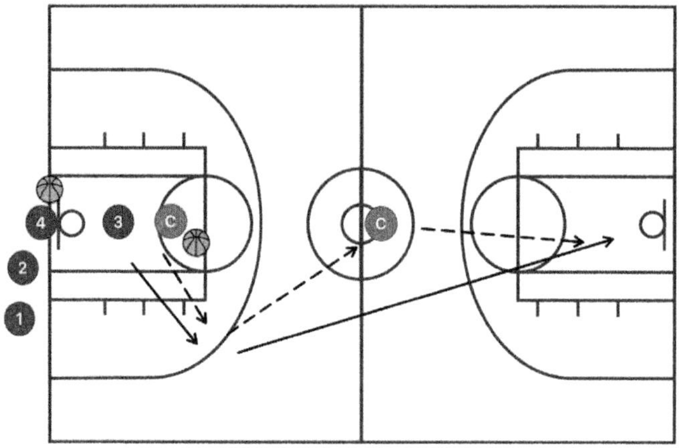

Why it's great

Halo passing is perfect for teaching your players how to handle loose balls in open court situations. Sometimes the passes won't be on target, but they'll still have to run the break, and this Team USA drill will teach just that.

Setup

Players line up under the baseline with balls. A coach stands at each free-throw line and at the center court.

Instructions

The player passes the ball to the coach at the free-throw line. They then receive the pass and throw it ahead to the coach at half-court. Cut to the basket and finish.

Coaching points

- Coaches should purposely throw bad passes – too low or too far in front.
- Despite these bad passes, players should not dribble the ball more than once.

Variation

- To get more players going in this drill, have the coaches stand on each sideline instead and run the drill down both halves of the court.

Dribble, pivot, pass

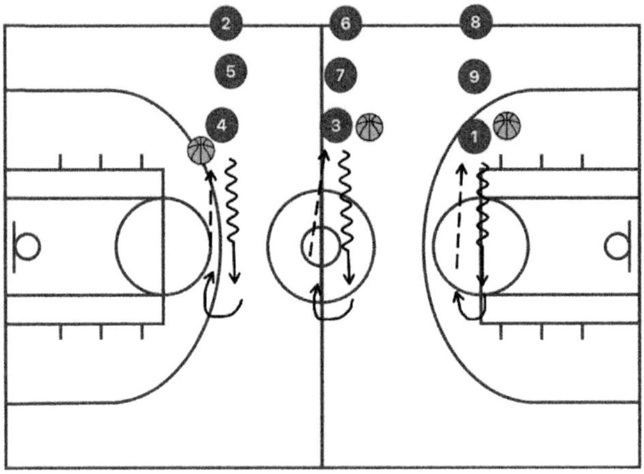

Why it's great

This drill is very similar to Bob Bigelow's fundamental passing drills. It's great evidence to your own players that the Team USA 17 players aren't 'too good' to reinforce the fundamentals.

Setup

Players line up three to a line. The front player has the ball.

Instructions

Players dribble 10 ft (3 m), then jump stop and pivot. Pass the ball to the first player and run to the end of the line.

Coaching points

- Players should rip the ball low, across the body, as they pivot and pass from that side.
- The key to this drill at this age is high intensity.

Three versus one passing

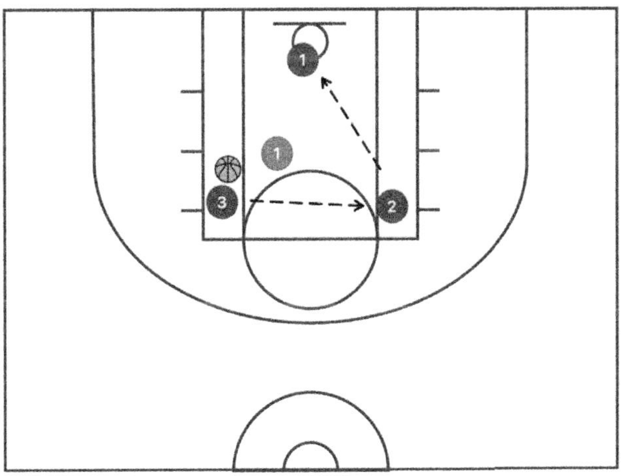

Why it's great

This drill focuses on passing in small-sided games and is suitable for all levels. You can increase the difficulty based on skill level.

Setup

In a confined space such as the key area, have three players against one defender.

Instructions

1. Defender tries to intercept the pass.
2. Offensive players can only pivot when they have the ball.
3. Passers can move without the ball.
4. Offensive players cannot step outside of the area.

Coaching points

The passers should use different passes to each other such as bounce, overhead, and behind the back moves.

Variations

Increase difficulty by:

- Changing the movable area.
- Adding another ball.
- Disallowing overhead passes.

Circle three-man weave

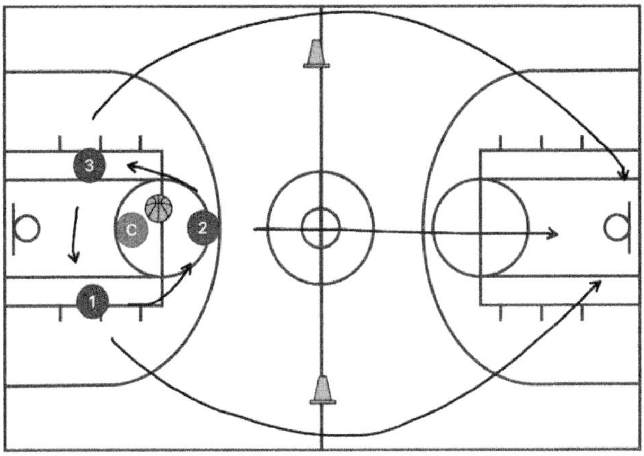

Why it's great

While we're not big fans of the traditional three-man weave, here's a modified version to teach your players to stay wide and pass the ball up the court quickly on a fast break.

Setup

The coach holds the ball and the players circle the coach. Place two cones one step away from the sidelines between the three-point and halfway line.

Instructions

Players jog around the coach, who will throw the ball to the backboard and the closest person has to get the rebound. One person has to receive the outlet pass while the other has to sprint to the outside of the cone. The rebounder passes to the outlet and also sprints to the outside of the cone. No dribbling, and pass the ball upcourt for a layup.

Variations

- Increase number of players from three to four or five. Let players self-organize on fast break.
- Add mental pressure by requesting that the players make 10 layups in a row without misses.

12

Conditioning drills

Conditioning drills are always the toughest part of practice, and if handled improperly they can become monotonous. Coaches need many drills up their sleeve to give their players different areas to improve their game in each practice.

We went through the data and found the 21 most popular conditioning drills on the Practice Planner. These drills are loved by your peers, so if you don't know them already that's a great reason to include them into your practice! They include:

- Fitness drills.
- Jump drills.
- Game-based drills.
- Gym drills.

Fitness drills

Sequence drill

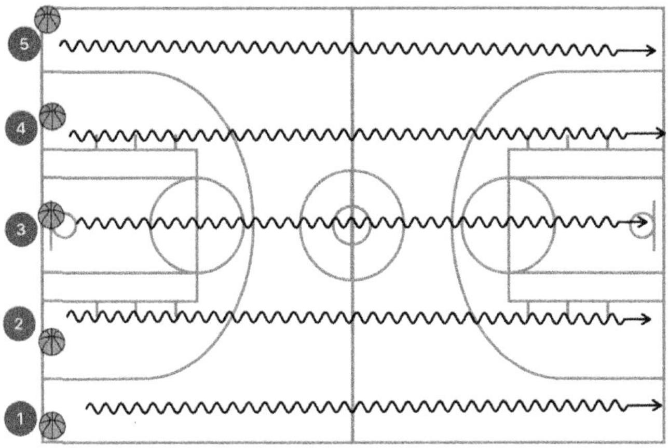

Why it's great

Coach Collins, three times state championship winner with Madison Memorial High School in Wisconsin, uses this drill to test his team at the start of the season. It shows you which players are tough and willing to give it their all.

Setup

Players line up along the baseline.

Instructions

Players must run one full length in five seconds. After a rest, they must run three lengths in 15 seconds. Repeat to run 1-3-5-7-9-11-13 lengths. After running 13 lengths, run 11-9-7-5-3-1 lengths.

Coaching points

- Make the drill more difficult by having players run while dribbling balls.
- Split the players into three groups – have the groups run through one by one and send the next group off when the first is finished. This is the rest interval.
- Run this drill only once a practice.

Toe touches

Why it's great

Toe touches are great for improving conditioning and foot speed, perfect for any circuit.

Setup

Players stand opposite a bench.

Instructions

At your call, players kick up and place one foot on top of the bench. Repeat at maximum intensity for 30 seconds.

Coaching points

- Bench height doesn't matter – it's all about the speed of the foot movement.
- Players should just touch the bench and not put any weight on it at all.

Stair sprints

Why this drill is great

This is a classic conditioning drill that can be done just about anywhere and will work the hamstrings, calves, and quads.

Setup

Players line up behind a set of stairs.

Instructions

Players run up the stairs, making sure to land on each step. At the top, walk back down. Run for 30 seconds.

Coaching points

- Players should drive the arms quickly to increase foot speed
- Get your team going up and down in a circular circuit for the most efficiency.

Box run relay

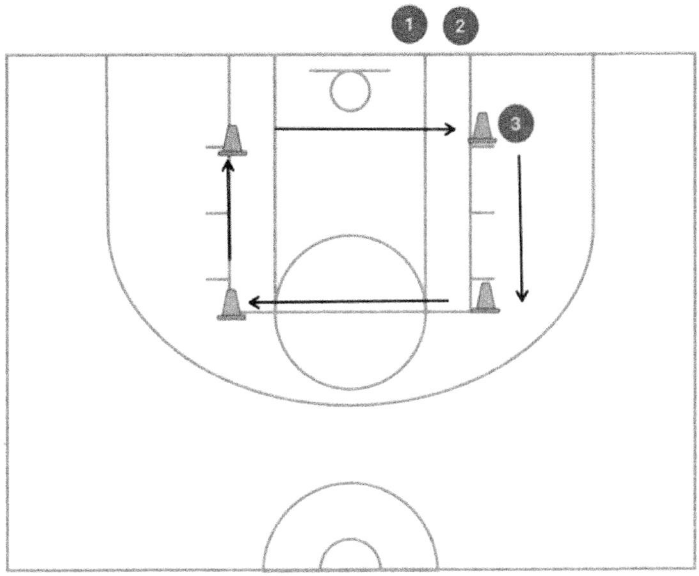

Why it's great

This agility drill develops quick movement in all directions and is a great basketball-specific conditioning drill for all ages.

Setup

Set up four cones in a 15 ft by 15 ft (4.5 m by 4.5 m) box, or alternatively place cones at the four corners of the key. Players line up behind a cone.

Instructions

At your call, players run forward to the first cone. They then shuffle sideways to the next, then backpedal, and finally shuffle sideways to the starting cone. Each player begins when the player in front of them has reached the first cone.

Coaching points

- Change the length of the rest interval by changing the number of players in line.
- Run the drill for five minutes or a number of laps.
- Remind younger players to not cross their legs when sliding laterally.

Hurdles series

Why it's great

This conditioning drill is a staple of drill stations as it works agility, footwork, and conditioning in a small space.

Setup

Set up a row of six–eight cones, each 1–2 ft (30–60 cm) apart. Line up four–six hurdles 2 ft (60 cm) apart in a line parallel to the cones. Players line up behind the cones.

Instructions

Players sidestep in a zigzag movement from cone to cone. At the top, they turn around and use both feet to jump over the hurdles to the end.

Coaching point

- Ensure that players aren't cheating in the sidestep – both feet need to be on one side of a cone before moving forward.
- Players should limit the amount of landing time before exploding into the next jump.
- Run the drill for three circuits.

Agility ladder series

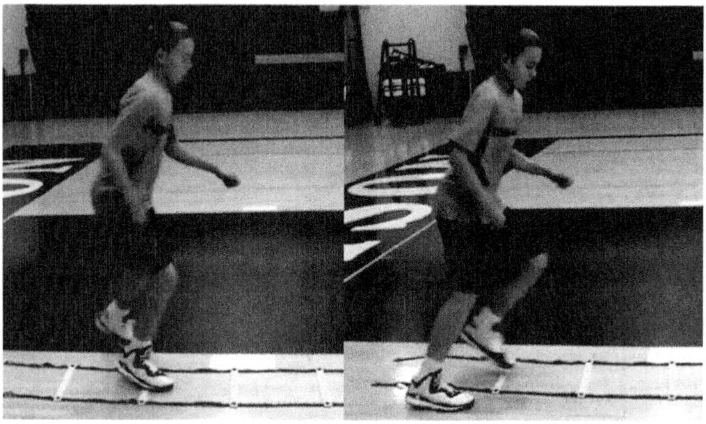

Why it's great

Coaches can use this drill to teach footwork and agility with the ball, particularly with the off-hand.

Setup

Place an agility ladder on the ground and place a cone at the end. Parallel to it, line up a row of six-eight cones 2 ft (60 cm) apart. Players line up behind the ladder holding basketballs.

Instructions

Players hop to the end of the ladder, alternating between jumping with both feet in and both feet out. At the end they begin dribbling. They dribble around the end cone and weave in and out of the others. Dribble with one hand.

Coaching points

- Place the cones closely together to make the drill more difficult.
- Vary the dribble moves at each cone to make the drill more difficult.
- Run the drill for three circuits.

Plyometric jump drills

Double leg linear drop to squat

Why it's great

Before you learn to jump, you must learn to land correctly. This exercise teaches your body how to absorb force from a height and be prepared to jump up again quickly. This quick second jump is a key skill of rebounding.

Setup

Players stand on the edge of a 12 in (30 cm) box with feet shoulder width apart.

Instructions

At your call, players quickly pick their feet off the box and land with both feet on the ground. Squat and hold the position for two seconds.

Coaching points

- Players should land on the mid-foot or balls of feet with the toes pointing upward.
- The chest must be kept tall with hips under shoulders.
- Try running for two sets of five.

Double leg linear repeating box jumps

Why it's great

This drills is the progression to the force absorption drill above. The goal is to immediately jump up following landing to maximize concentric contraction to grow muscle and induce some fatigue.

Setup

Line up three–four boxes one in front of the other, with a 2 ft (60 cm) gap between them. Players face the box.

Instructions

At your call, players jump up onto the first box. They then move to the edge and step off it with one foot, landing on both feet. Repeat through the rest of the boxes.

Coaching points

- Players must immediately jump up after landing, but also be aware to land with the correct technique.
- Knees must be kept in line with the hips when landing and jumping.
- Try running for two sets of five.

Double leg continuous rotational cone jumps

Why it's great

This drills is part of the third and final progression of the above two drills, developing body control in the air (great for finishing) and further increasing game-ready endurance.

Setup

Set up four-six cones in a straight line with 1-2 ft (30-60 cm) between each. Players face the line of cones.

Instructions

At your call, players jump as high as possible over each cone. Upon landing, they jump up quickly over the next, rotating 90 degrees in the air. Land on both feet. Repeat rotating in the other direction.

Coaching points

- If players are struggling with this drill, have them practice just rotating 90 degrees in the air and landing on a box.
- Try running for four sets of three.

Hop jump

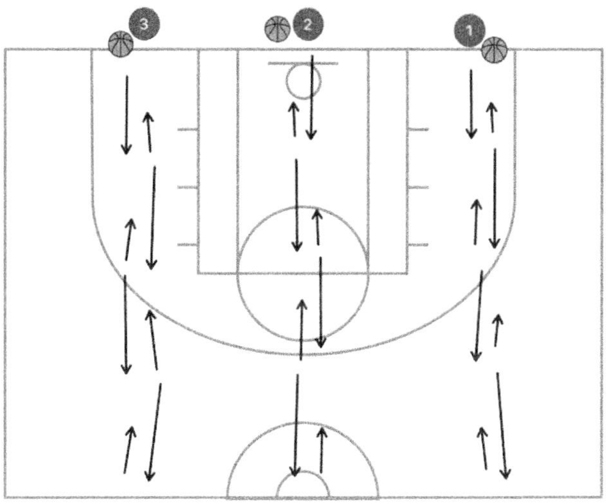

Why it's great

This drill is a great warm-up drill for your players to get them to work on an explosive second jump to grab rebounds.

Setup

Players line up along the baseline.

Instructions

At your call, players take a large jump forward. Land with both feet and then take a small jump backward. Repeat to half-court.

Game-based drills

Slide sprint layup

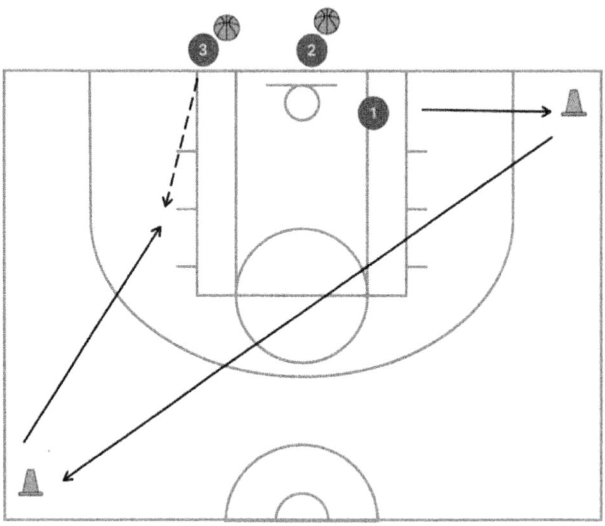

Why it's great

This drill was designed by Brian McCormick, the game-based training guru. It is a great way to get your players fit while reinforcing layups skills.

Setup

Players line up under the basket along the baseline.

Instructions

Players slide along the baseline to the corner. At the corner, they sprint to the opposite half-court corner. From there they cut to the basket, catch a pass, and layup.

Coaching points

- Have your players run so that they start when the player in front has finished sliding.
- To increase the game-based element, players cannot finish in the same way as the player in front of them – i.e. if a player does a normal one-two right-handed layup, the next player can't do the same.

Five spot toughness drill

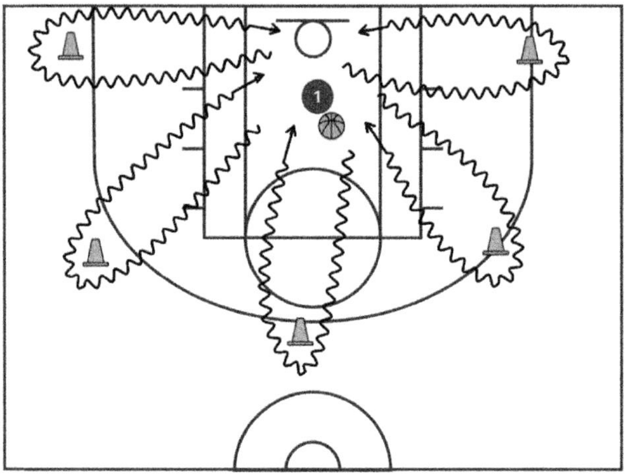

Why it's great

Layup lines can be too repetitive – this drill gets the player attacking the basket from different angles and will ensure players can finish when tired at the end of the game.

Setup

Place five cones along the perimeter, one at the top, one at each wing, and one at each elbow extended. A rebounder stands under the basket with the ball, and the player starts under the basket.

Instructions

The player runs from under the basket to the cone at the wing. They circle around it and cut to the basket, catching the ball and laying up. Repeat on each cone around the perimeter.

Coaching points

- An advanced progression involves players running to the cone pointed at by the coach.
- Players should pair up and can perform this group with other pairs on the same hoop.

Defensive slide with resistance band

Why it's great

You can do this drill at home – it won't wake the neighbors so you have no excuse to not get better!

Setup

Stand in a defensive stance with a resistance band looped around your ankles.

Instructions

Slide laterally, slowly, moving one outer foot then the other inner foot.

Coaching points

- Focus on the push-pull of the defensive stance. Hold the resistance band at the point when it is furthest apart for one second before sliding to your normal stance.
- Keep your knees slightly bent throughout the drill.

Backboard taps with resistance

Why it's great

This drill involves the ball but also provides extra resistance that will help players develop the lower-body strength to fight for rebounds.

Setup

Players are attached to a resistance band and stand under the basket holding a ball. The coach holds down a resistance band at the top of the perimeter.

Instructions

Players hold the ball with two hands and jump up with both feet, aiming to touch the backboard with the ball.

Coaching points

- Players need to hold the ball at chin height, elbows out, to practice protecting the ball following rebounding.
- Run the drill for three sets of 10.

Gym drills

Side plank

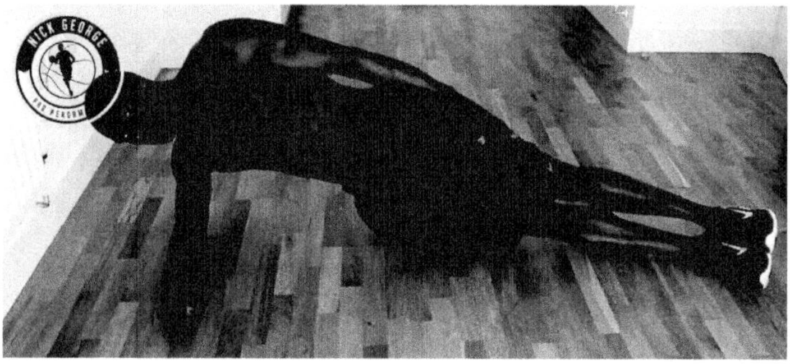

Why it's great

The side plank works on the often overlooked oblique and lower back muscles that are needed for core stability and for preventing injury.

Setup

Players lie sideways on the ground, balancing on a bent elbow.

Instructions

At the start of the exercise, players elevate off the ground, keeping one foot on the other and the body in a straight line. Hold for 30 seconds and then repeat on both sides.

Coaching points

- Keep the elbow directly beneath the shoulders throughout the exercise.
- Don't let the hip drop.
- A more difficult variation involves raising the upper leg.

Star cones

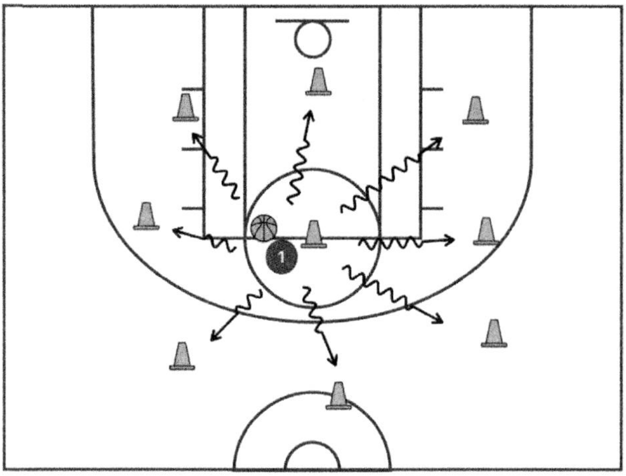

Why it's great

This is a useful drill because it very closely resembles what happens in games: short intense bursts of speed in multiple directions.

Setup

Set up cones in a circle with a cone in the middle.

Instructions

The coach can label each cone or point in the direction of each cone. The player must start from the middle and then quickly sprint and touch the outside cone.

Three spot cones

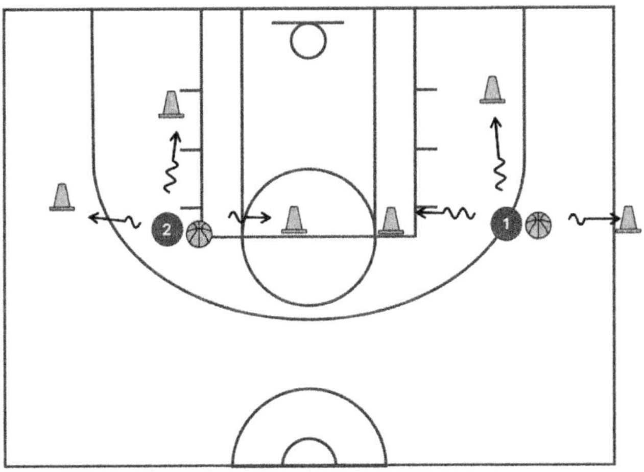

Why it's great

This is an advanced abs exercise that gets great results. All serious athletes should be able to perform a set of these under control.

Setup

Grip a chin-up with your legs hanging straight down.

Instructions

Players raise their legs up to 90 degrees and hold them there for one count. Repeat for 10–12 reps in three sets.

Coaching points

- Keep the legs straight throughout and bend at the hip.
- The grip should be held slightly wider than shoulder length.

Ball roll push-ups

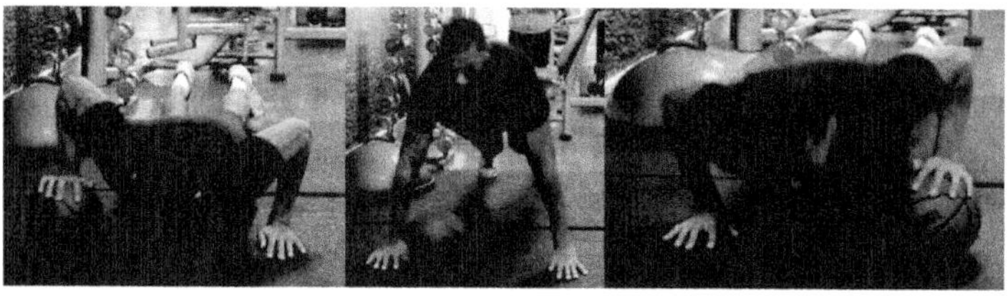

Why it's great

Plyometric push-ups build power, strength, and explosiveness in the chest and shoulders, all without equipment.

Setup

Players get into a push-up stance, with their hands apart slightly wider than their shoulders.

Instructions

Players perform a regular push-up. At the base, they push up quickly and take their hands slightly off the ground. Land and repeat for 10 reps in four sets.

Coaching points

- Players need to be looking slightly forward throughout this exercise.
- It is important to keep the back straight and abdominal muscles tightened.
- A variation involves bringing the hands closer together to target the triceps.

Catch me if you can

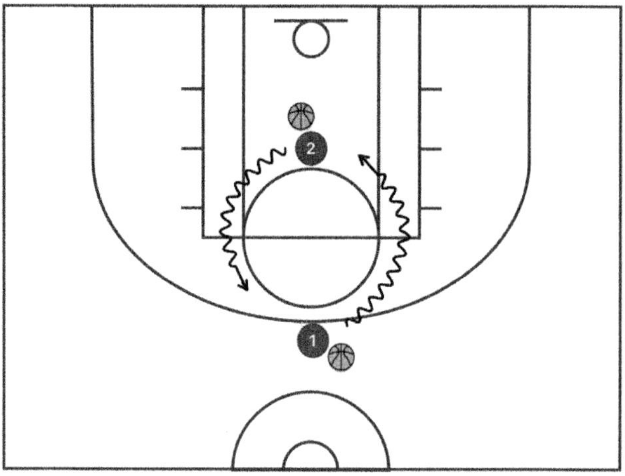

Why it's great

This drill works on the many change of direction and pace movements during a basketball game.

Setup

Have two players facing each other outside of the free throw line circle, and designate one person as the catcher.

Instructions

When coach says go, one person has to try to catch the other person. Both players must run along the outside of the circle. Give them a time limit of 10–30 seconds. The chaser can change directions and both players must dribble a ball.

Coaching points

- Focus on keeping eyes up and dribble low.

Knees and shoulder game

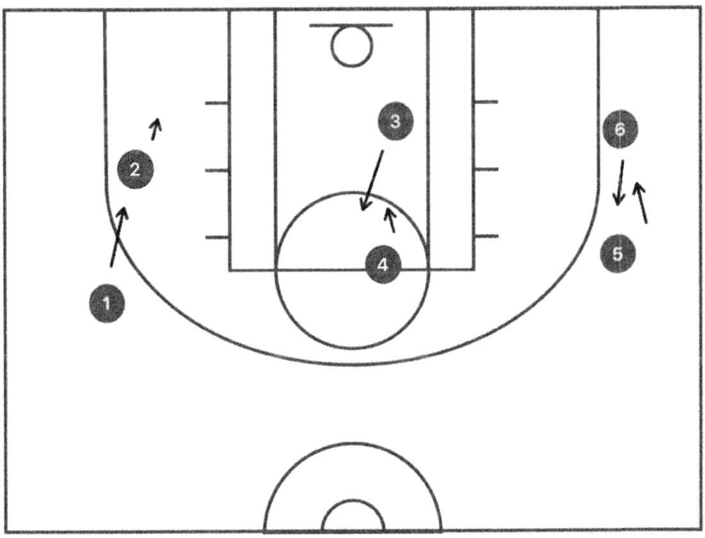

Why it's great

This is a great drill to work on change of direction and spatial awareness that simulates real game situations.

Setup

Have 2 players face each other about arm's length distance away.

Instructions

- You score a point if you touch your opponent's shoulder or knee.
- Play up to 10 points.

Coaching points

- Staying low in a defensive stance helps players change directions quicker.

Medicine ball dribbling

Why it's great

This combo drill works on both strength and dribbling. It's also quite fun because it's different. Because of the uneven weight distribution, it also helps to build stabilization when dribbling.

Instructions

While pound dribbling hard, pick up and throw the medicine ball onto the ground. Do it 10 times on each hand. You can increase the difficulty by:

- Doing a crossover between each medicine ball throw.
- Doing a behind the back move between each medicine ball throw.

Wall squat with ball throw

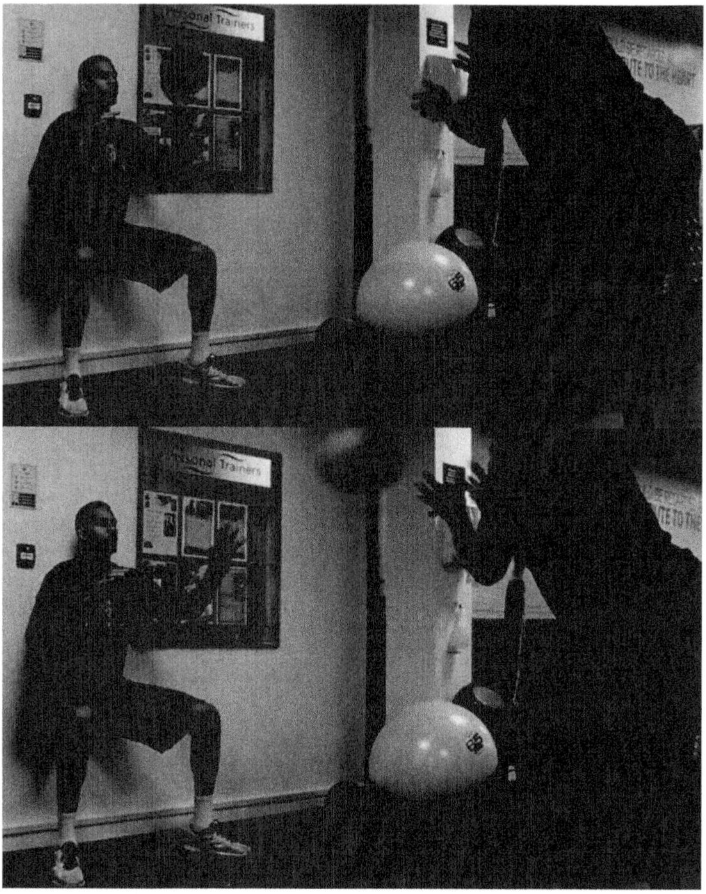

Why it's great

This is a really good team building exercise. It works on all the muscles required in a defensive stance and adds variability by forcing the players to react to the ball.

Instructions

Ask all the players to sit along a wall. The coach can hold a medicine ball or basketball and randomly throw it to a player who must catch and return the ball with one hand.

Cone core plank game

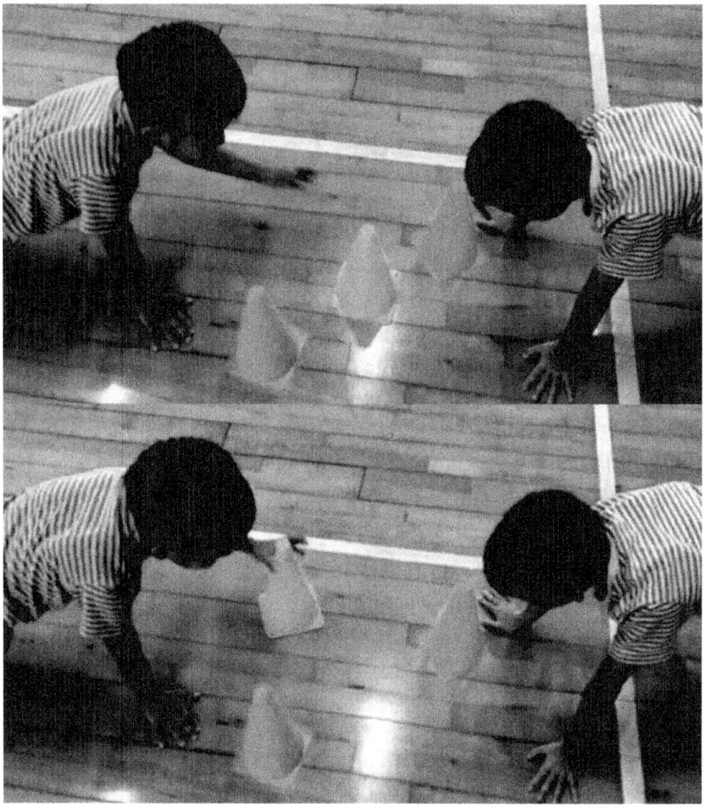

Why it's great

A fun game that works on both balance and core strength.

Instructions

In pairs, place three cones in the middle and go into a plank position. One player grabs a cone then the other has to grab one too. Then the first person grabs a cone again and puts one back. Keep going until one person's knees touches the ground.

Tic-tac-toe game

Why it's great

A fun game that works on conditioning, decision making and dribbling.

Instructions

- Using hula hoops, form a tic tac toe square at one end of the court. At the other hand, have two teams with three pinnies each.

- One person from each team can dribbling to the hula hoops and place a pinny into a hoop.
- The first team to have three pinnies in a row wins.
- If all pinnies have been placed inside the hoops, players can relocate one existing pinny to a new location.

One-on-one full court

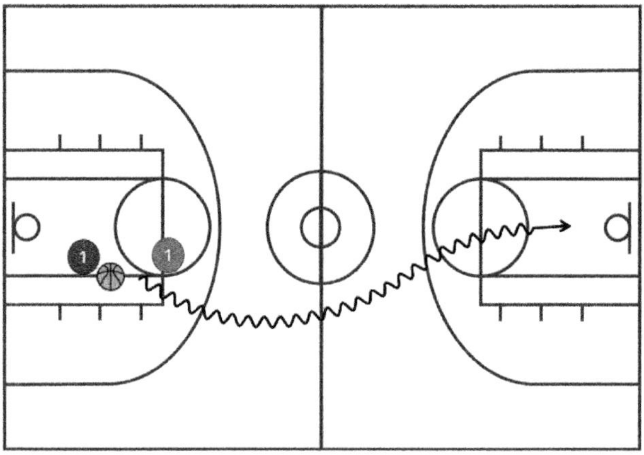

Why it's great

The ultimate toughness drill. This drill is used by many famous coaches and even at the professional level. Works on one-on-one and also conditioning.

Instructions

Play one-on-one full court no out of bounds. Offense stays if they score, but if defense gets a rebound then offense comes off and a new defender comes on.

13

Practice plans for ages 6-9

At the age of six to nine years old, you'll probably be introducing basketball to kids for the first time. It is at this age that they will start to develop what will hopefully become a lifelong passion for the game. I'm a big fan of Canada Basketball's Long-Term Athlete Development (LTAD) model and this chapter is largely based on that.

If there's one thing to take away from this chapter, it's to make practice FUN and ENCOURAGING.

Here's a crazy statistic: 70 percent of children are dropping out of organized sports by the age of 13. The reason? It's just not fun anymore. The problem with quitting early is that you'll never know if a kid will have a growth spurt later on and become a great player. Less participation also means a smaller pool of players to choose from for the next level, and this affects the quality of the national and professional teams.

I know that coaches all have a competitive drive and want to win games, but at this level you have to let go of your ego. You need to accept that there's a chance that nobody's ever going to acknowledge that you're a great coach because you can't prove it with wins and accolades. What you do get is the satisfaction of seeing these kids growing in character and building up their confidence, which in my opinion is worth a lot more.

Here you can learn more about what specific pointers you need to take with you into practice, or you can turn to page 261 to find complete practice plan templates we've prepared for you.

Things to cover in order of importance

1. The desire to have fun and develop an interest in sport.
2. ABCs – agility, balance, and coordination.
3. Ball sense and spatial awareness.
4. Footwork.
5. Layups.
6. Shooting form.
7. Dribbling.
8. Passing.
9. Rules of the game, as well as the concept of attack and defense.

Basic team offense and defense concepts – plan your practices

> *"I would spend almost as much time planning a practice as conducting it. Everything was planned out each day."*
> *– John Wooden (1910–2010), head coach at UCLA*

Legendary coach John Wooden – the 'Wizard of Westwood' – would write out his practices on index cards, which can be a great idea. You've only got your kids for an hour or so each day, so you need to make maximum use of that time. By planning, you prepare yourself for every practical eventuality. What if there aren't enough balls, or the kids find the drills too challenging, or your assistant coach is sick? Even though you might be a volunteer, practice planning puts you right up there with the professionals in my book.

When you're not worried about what drill to run next, you can spend your time encouraging your players.

Pick your equipment carefully:

- Use a smaller ball.
- Lower the rim.
- Get as many baskets as possible.
- Have one ball for each person.

Strength is a key issue at this age. It is extremely difficult for young kids to shoot a full-sized basketball into a regular hoop. Just imagine yourself bouncing and shooting a 9 lb (4.1 kg) ball at the age of six – it's tough!

Remember the physical and mental limitations at this age and be conscious of how much strength and stamina kids have. For example, instead of dribbling standing up you can ask them to get on one knee or sit on a chair to give it a go. Always have different levels of difficulty of each drill for the varying levels of skill and strength.

General pointers for sticking to this include limiting drills to fit shorter attention spans, and sticking to one or two areas (encourage passing above all). Remember that kids aren't strong enough to shoot so don't worry about it too much – it's better to teach basic motor skills over results.

Maximize time on task. This is simply the time spent on actually doing something with the ball. Most practices have less than 50 percent of the time spent on actually moving or touching the ball as the coach is often talking and the players are standing in line watching. Preparing for practice can help increase the time spent on tasks by cutting down on explanation and transition time.

Use games that require a ball per player, having lots of baskets to shoot at, and playing two-on-two or three-on-three instead of five-on-five to maximize touches. If you don't know where to begin we've got two practice plans here for you to choose from.

For absolute beginners, we recommend using Coach Bigelow's practice plans. For example, it's difficult to play dribble tag when you've never touched a ball before. Coach Bigelow is an expert at kid's basketball and he breaks down skills into child-friendly exercises, such as rolling the ball on the floor and ball wraps around the body.

For kids that are starting to master the skills, we recommend Coach Brian McCormick's game-based practices. They'll find the games fun and challenging, and they are also surprisingly easy to pick up, as they're all based on games that they will already know, such as tag or monkey in the middle.

The first practice plan is by Bob Bigelow and the second practice plan is by Brian McCormick.

My recommended template is three to five minutes of class introduction. Prepare students mentally for this by including 15 minutes of warm-up and SAQ (strength, agility, and quickness). Do 15-20 minutes of technical skills work,15-20 minutes of small-sided games, and two or three minutes finishing the class. After you have finished hold a brief Q&A session with students.

Bob Bigelow practice plan template is as follows:
Warm-up drills - 10 minutes.
Ball around body warm-up exercises.
Spin, catch, jump stop, and pivot drill.

Finishing drills - 20 minutes.
Layup drill with no ball.
Layup drill off wall.
Layup drill at the basket.

Break - 10 minutes.

Passing drills - 20 minutes.
One-hand wall pass.
Square passing.
Three-on-three scrimmage.

Brian McCormick practice plan template is as follows:
Warm-up - 10 minutes.
Rock, paper, scissors tag.

Two ball together.
Two ball high low.
Two ball side-to-side.
Protect the dribble.

Dribbling drills – 15 minutes.
Box tag.
Tag team dribbling.

Break – five minutes.

Team offense and passing – 30 minutes.
Long Island passing drill.
Tag ball passing drill with three-player advantage.
Two-on-two rugby drill.
Three-on-three scrimmage.

14

Practice plans for ages 11-14

"The single most important aspect of coaching is running effective practices."
– Bob Knight

One of the things I regret the most was showing up to practice and winging it early in my coaching career. I'd just rely on drills my old coach used back in the 1980s. Yes, I should have figured that the game has changed a lot since then!

Here are the problems with NOT planning ahead:

- Setting a bad example. I'm trying to teach life skills and being prepared is a great ability to impart.
- Time wasted. If you count the hours you have during the season and think about all the things you want to cover, there's simply not a lot of time. Every minute counts.
- Boring practices. It's tough to come up with new ideas on the spot so most likely you'll end up repeating the same

drills over and over again. When I first started out as a coach my players were bored.
- Not training with a purpose. Every drill should have a purpose, whether it's adding something to your offensive system or fixing a problem from the last game. Without planning, the drills don't tie in with what happens in game.

It's hard to start from scratch so here are three templates you can use:
- Two-hour middle school practice plan.
- Two-hour AAU practice plan.
- Two-hour game-based practice plans.

Middle school practice plan

Warm-up drills – 10 minutes.
Hop jump.
Kangaroo warm-up.
Lunge reach.
Open gate.
Full-court off-hand.
Four-man weave.

Rebounding drills – 20 minutes.
Box jumps put backs.
Youth rebounding.
Break – five minutes.

Shooting drills – 20 minutes.
Bounce shooting.
3-2-1 Shooting.
Full-court shooting drill
90-second shotgun drill.
Break – five minutes.

Small-sided games – 10 minutes.
Full-court scrimmage.

AAU specific practice plan
Warm-up – 10 minutes.
High knees.
Toe touches.
Jog and sprints.
Three-man weave.

Defense drills – 20 minutes.
Closeout drill.
Shark water.
Break – 5 minutes.

Team defense drills – 20 minutes.
Five-on-five shell defense.
Five-on-four backside cutter drill.
Four-on-four baseline drive rotation.
Break – five minutes.

Full-court scrimmage – 10 minutes.

Game-based practice plan

Warm-up – 10 minutes.
Box tag.
Foster one-on-one drill.
Two-on-two rugby drill.

Transition offense drills – 20 minutes.
Two-man chaser layups.
Two-on-two army drill.
Tip transition drill.
Break – five minutes.

Half-court offense drills – 20 minutes.
Team passing tag.
Five person string shooting with three-on-two.
Four-on-four Canada rules.
Break – five minutes.

Full-court scrimmage – 10 minutes.

Don Kelbick player development practice plan
Turn out layups – make 15 in a row.
Turn out jump shots – make seven in a row.
Turn out/rip/one dribble – make 15 in a row.
Free throws (break) – seven in a row.
Turn out second dribble change – make 20 in three minutes.
Turn out/second dribble change/crossover – make 20 in total.
Turn out/double change/jump shot – make seven in a row.
Free throws (break) – make 20 total.
Sweep/one dribble/jump shot – make 10.
Two dribble jump shot – make five in a row.
Two dribble/change/jump shot – make 10.

Free throws (break) 10 points – +1 per make, -2 per miss.

Final thoughts

I hope you've enjoyed this book – it is the kind of guide I certainly wish I had read when I first started coaching. One of the most important lessons that I've learnt from talking with the great coaches featured in these pages is that they all have a deep thirst for learning. I've seen many famous coaches writing notes when listening to other coaches speak. They're experts because they've accumulated more knowledge than you and I, and at a faster rate.

This book presents many contradicting ideas that will hopefully challenge your way of thinking, maybe to its core. As I learned from Team USA U17 head coach Don Showalter, your coaching is a reflection of who you are and you must choose a style that suits you. Everyone is different and that's why I admire coaches with a strong philosophy behind their methods.

A lot of the drills in this book are about putting your players in a random environment to induce them to grow and improve. I truly believe the best way to lead is by example. The ideas and drills presented here may fail horribly at your next practice session, but mistakes are good as long as you adapt and learn from them. I've tried more than a few drills that went horribly wrong, but for the majority of time my experiments turn out for the better.

The future of basketball lies in your hands. There's nothing more satisfying than seeing your players grow. I hope you are excited to try these ideas and drills at your next practice session – trust me, I've tried them all and your players will love you for it.

– Keith Rumjahn

Printed in Great Britain
by Amazon

20572163R00159